CREATED AND PHOTOGRAPHED BY ALIX GOLDSMITH

WITH TEST ANALYSES BY MICHEL RADOMISLI, PH.D.,

Clinical Associate Professor at Cornell University Medical College—New York Hospital, Payne Whitney Clinic

A FIRESIDE BOOK PUBLISHED BY SIMON & SCHUSTER

NEW YORK LONDON TORONTO SYDNEY TOKYO SINGAPORE

CELEBRITEST

FIRESIDE

Simon & Schuster Building

Rockefeller Center

1230 Avenue of the Americas

New York, New York 10020

DESIGNED BY BONNI LEON

Photograph on page 175 is courtesy of Colm Henry

Manufactured in the United States of America

10 9 8 7 6 5 4 3 2 1

Library of Congress Cataloging-in-Publication Data

Goldsmith, Alix.
    Celebritest/created and photographed by Alix
Goldsmith; with test analyses by Michel Radomisli.
        p.   cm.
      1. Celebrities—United States—Interviews.
2. Celebrities—United States—Psychology.
3. Celebrities—United States—Protraits.
I. Radomisli, Michel.   II. Title.
CT2220.G62   1991
920.073—dc20   981-4105 CIP

ISBN 0-671-67442-0

To my parents and Goffredo for their support

throughout this adventure.

And of course, to the seventy exceptional people who

lent me their personalities and enthusiasm for a few

hours and made this book possible.

—A.G.

SPECIAL THANKS TO

Susan Blond

Susan McNally

Dany Jucand

Ramsy and Alaïa Salem

Elisabeth Dalling

Sam Richards

Dan Aykroyd

Sabrina Guiness

Priscilla Elwes

Damian and Christina Elwes

Paul McGuiness

John and Pat Tigrett

Loretta Roccanova

Ed Epstein

Louis-Charles de Remusat

Johnny Pigozzi

Sheila Rosh

Anne Crawford

Nancy and Andrew Jarecki

New York, 1988. I find myself at the book-launching party of a good friend. Since I don't know many guests at the party, my host kindly introduces me to the New York publishing world. My friend's editor is there, and we start talking. He tells me about a few of his current projects, and I bring him up to date on my latest endeavor. A book of drawings . . . tests really, that I went around and collected from politicians, artists, businessmen, sports figures, and others in Paris, accompanied by my photographs of these people. He appears interested, so I describe the test to him.

I tell him that it consists of a rectangle divided into six squares of equal size. Each square represents something (though the respondents are not told this until later). Within each square is a sign. First, a dot; second, a circle; third, a square; fourth, a little line; fifth, a curved line; sixth, a dotted line. I ask them to draw whatever comes to mind . . . to use each box as they see fit. Then I ask them to write down what the drawing represents to them in a word, title, sentence—however they like. They date and sign the test, and I go on to explain the meaning of each square. The first is how you see yourself; the second, how you see others; third, relations, couples; the fourth is life; the fifth, sexuality; the sixth, imagination. Once they know the meaning of each square, I ask them to tell me if they find any connection between the drawing and what they know of themselves—if it is significant to them in some way and whether it might relate to their philosophy of life.

As I finish describing my unusual endeavor, the editor says "Please send me a copy. I would love to see this." As soon as I get back to Paris, I send the book off to Simon & Schuster. To my great surprise, a week later a letter arrives. Would I be interested in doing an American version?

Two months later, luggage in hand, I arrive back in the Big Apple, but this time not so much for recreation as research. After promising the editor that I could secure these "interviews" and corresponding drawings from everyone from Armand Hammer to Michael Douglas, my contract is signed! Now it strikes me that somehow I am going to have to make good on these outrageous promises.

The first step was to approach the people I thought would be appropriate—but how to get close enough to these busy people to ask them to participate? I go into high gear, tracking down every current or former friend I can think of who might help in my quest. The friends I managed to lasso came through for me, and the process began. Once I met a few of the personalities, I realized that if I approached them carefully, they were generally willing to play along.

Michael Douglas is the first person I interview. A week later Ahmet Ertegun consents. A funky Nile Rodgers laughs away. Jay McInerney follows. I visit Oscar de la Renta soon after. New York is opening its doors! Sting's manager Ian Copeland greets me in his office. I meet Bret Easton Ellis and Tama Janowitz in their downtown apartments, Milton Glaser in his design center. Writer Fran Lebowitz speeds through the test over coffee. Then I'm off to visit Peter Marino, the architect, and Jerzy Kosinski, who types out all the answers (well—why not!). Malcolm Forbes, dynamic and young-spirited, takes me around the Forbes Museum and then to lunch at Mortimer's. At the end of lunch he hands me a scarf emblazoned with his motto: Capitalist Tool. Love it!

Meeting Mary McFadden is like going back in time. Egypt, Africa, Ancient Greece, and Rome came to my mind. Mary is a true collector, and entering her office is like walking into the cavern of Ali Baba. From beautiful gowns, to sculptures from her days in Africa, to her photographs and garden designs. Only a woman could give such a feeling of home to her office.

Lawyer Richard Golub is recommended to me as a controversial New Yorker. A serene Indian butler opens the door and lets me in, presenting himself as Mr. K. "Please, Miss, Mr. Golub is waiting for you. Go upstairs to the third floor." I am suddenly propelled into another world; oriental paintings, rugs, statues . . . I enter the room and find Golub, to my surprise and embarrassment, lying on his bed, speaking on the phone. Mr. K. breaks the ice: "So, young lady is here to bring pleasure to my master?" I respond shakily, "No, not really—that may be his next appointment . . ."

Finally the test starts, finishes, and off we go to lunch. I really find myself liking this somewhat misunderstood character. The next day, Golub calls to tell me he returned home to find a bat caught in his sitting room curtains—seemed a fitting end to our encounter.

After the Golub interview, to my horror, my luck turns. Just an endless string of answers like "Maybe," "I don't know," "No time right now," and "Who are you anyway?" Help!

I decide to try my hand in Los Angeles. It's April, two nights before Oscar night. I enlist three great girlfriends. In less than two weeks they take me everywhere, organize dinners with actor friends, directors, hoping that some will agree. One night, with the girls as hosts, the whole dinner table took my test! At this dinner, Julian Sands and actors Cecilia Peck and Valeria Golino became my first subjects in L.A.

James Spader stops by one day to visit a friend who is out, but I'm not! Poor thing, a rather quiet Spader takes the test. Wondering, "Who is she? What is she doing here? Where are my friends?" Driving to Harry Dean Stanton's was a seemingly endless journey—with me not yet used to LA's urban sprawl—up winding canyon roads with the most beautiful spread of mountains in front of me, going on forever without a house in sight. Finally I reach the oasis of Harry Dean, eating breakfast in his robe, very cool indeed!

The venue for my meeting with Charlie Sheen—Harry's Bar—seemed an interesting choice for someone who proclaims himself to be "on the wagon." He is in his dark, brooding mood— intense is the least I can say as I read his poetry and look at the drawings that accompany each poem. He really gets into the test, and he is so sweet that he finally ends up asking his father to take it as well. Martin agrees! (To my dismay, Martin's test was later stolen along with the one I did with artist Keith Haring.)

For my photos of him, Marcus Allen takes me to his gym in a Ferrari.

Alan Parker is the only person to have been caught twice, appearing in this book and the one I published in France three years earlier. The first three squares of each test are the same, but the last three have metamorphosed. My first encounter with Alan was in Cannes the year he was representing *Birdy*. We met at Clint Eastwood's party for his film *Pale Rider*. Eastwood was trying to wangle his way out of taking the test: "I'll do it if Alan does it!" he says. As I try to force my way through the horde of journalists, I am certain the cause is lost. To my surprise, I suddenly hear, "Oh, I love your shoes." Alan Parker had noticed my painted polkadot Jackson Pollock shoes. So, ten minutes later, Eastwood and Parker are sitting down like schoolboys, sketching away. Next day, their photo session on a 100-foot yacht. The second meeting is in LA just as *Mississippi Burning* is released by the ever-controversial Mr. Parker.

Administering the test to Timothy Leary, the icon of the revolutionary '60s, is a great thrill. Meeting Kirk Douglas is like plunging back into my childhood. He is just as I expected: a complete gentleman, and he does the test with elegance. I find Charlton Heston and Roger Moore at a tennis tournament in Monte Carlo, where both consent to take the test. In two minutes Heston scribbles the eleventh commandment. Frank Sinatra is also there but unapproachable. Joan Collins is on hand to congratulate the winners, and I get up my courage to ask her. After declaring "No interviews today!" to every member of the press, she quietly sips her champagne in the sun and takes the test. (I was thrilled at the time, but unfortunately Joan later declined to have her test included in the collection).

With these prize interviews in hand, I head back to LA for a meeting with photographer Peter Beard. The floor of the acupuncturist's office where we conduct our interview is littered with Beard's pens and ink bottles. Later I photograph him as he leaps into the pool of the Sunset Marquis Hotel, wine glass in hand. With Peter's charm, the doused sunbathers can only forgive his exuberance. My friend, Euva—Queen of Kitsch and free spirit—introduces me to Lauren Hutton, and I interview both. Lauren stays in Euva's twenties Pink Palace in LA. I spend a whole afternoon running after Lauren to make sure she finishes the last square. Lauren is the eternal teenager, so beautiful and fresh. I find that Bob Rafaelson is a harder catch. A secretive man with a deep dislike for public appearances and Hollywood glitz, he turned in a most interesting test. As if getting Rafaelson to sit still for that long was not enough of a chore, I join the crew of rock legend Robbie Robertson's latest video as an assistant and catch him off guard.

After leaving a couple of messages, I finally connect with Julian Lennon in November 1989, strapped down in his seat on a plane to London with ten hours ahead of us and lots of time to draw; he was a good sport about it. Johnny Lydon, alias Johnny Rotten, is the most amusing and refreshing person in London. Sitting in a corner of his colorful, cheery house, surrounded with yellow silk curtains is Johnny, full of life, which completely changes my preconception of the King of the Punk Movement.

On my return to New York, I visit painter Kenny Scharf's house, thirty minutes outside Manhattan. I find myself climbing a strange staircase, where hang huge paintings depicting little creatures in flying saucers and which leads to rooms full of his creations. By this time I have realized that each switch, TV, phone, fridge, microwave is carefully camouflaged with hundreds of plastic items: everything from fake vegetation to little houses, boxes, people, animals, cover his household appliances. I am transfixed, and by the time we finish the interview, the car is covered by three feet of snow!

I race to meet Diane von Furstenberg, who does the test half an hour before leaving for Europe. She lets me into her world of beauty, grace, and femininity—surprising for such a successful businesswoman. The interview goes by too quickly.

Back to LA. This time with another science fiction buff, Dan Aykroyd, who does a beautiful test . . . and all in color. Two days after our interview, Dan calls me on the phone. "Hi, Alix. Why don't you come over to the set. Kim Basinger is here." I can't believe my ears—great! I get to Dan's trailer, he is there with his friend Jon Lovitz, a fellow cast member from *My Stepmother Is an Alien.* We immediately persuade him to take the test, and Dan seems to be even more excited to see his friend's results than I am. The somewhat perverse results seem to show the man's got a one-track mind! Kim arrives, and with Dan raving about how much he liked taking the test, we go off to her trailer. She immediately starts her drawings while I sit down and look around. As soon as I start giving her the meaning of each square, she starts screaming with laughter. So refreshing. Time to back on the set. I go and watch Dan and Kim perform, and I even get to give the test to Dan's wife, Donna Dixon.

Soon after this I am invited to David Hockney's house. His drawings in the test are beautiful, of course, and we spend a wonderful afternoon exploring his studio. I go home feeling so lucky to have his sketches in the book. A few days later, to my horror, his test is nowhere to be found! I turn my house upside down. I don't have the courage to call him. Months later a friend walks in with my missing briefcase. He had sold his car and the new owner called to return the bag found in the trunk, which happened to contain the test. Thank you, God.

After my meeting with Armand Hammer in his tremendous, imposing offices, I am happy to report that at the age of 93, this billionaire was still wonderfully flitratious and the only man in the book to really flirt with me!

So that's how much of this happened. I hope you will have as much fun reading this as I did putting it all together, tracking the celebrities, convincing them to take the test, and capturing them on film. Part of the fun was the spontaneity of it: always being ready at a moment's notice, test in hand and camera equipment in the car. The most enjoyable meetings were often the ones which I did not anticipate. Not knowing when I would stumble into a celebrity made those meetings all the more fun. Once at the LA night club El Dorado, I unexpectedly ran into The Edge (from the group U2). As I began politely and naively trying to schedule a convenient time to get together for the test, he surprised me with his response: "Now or never." I immediately ripped a concert poster off the wall and used the back for the test form. It was these instances that made it worthwhile.

After this two-year fantastic journey, I find myself miraculously with the material for a book on my hands. Somehow, this cacophony of personalities took shape and it began to appear as though there had been some logic to this whole thing—and that the tests and analyses, taken as a whole, managed to end up greater than the sum of their parts. I had learned a great deal about a large number of interesting people. I had seen them at home, at work, and under their cars. They were all quite wonderfully different. But by giving them all the test—the great equalizer—and learning from each of their responses to this same challenge, I had been able to see their most interesting and personal sides. Here was not the public persona, not the carefully constructed image honed by years of careful image building and spin doctoring by seasoned publicists and agents.

Here suddenly was a picture of unaccommodated celebrity—a simple portrait, frame by frame, of the inner workings of seventy exceptional people.

Alix Goldsmith

New York, 1991

Tests are everywhere. Tests are also irresistible. Look at any display of popular magazines. Their covers announce tests that tell you whether you are taking good care of your skin, or how outgoing you are, or whether your marriage is in trouble and it is time to seek professional help, and an amazing number of other things about yourself.

A *psychological* test is one that attempts some description of a person's "mind." Different psychologists define "mind" in different ways; they talk about "traits" versus "states," about aptitudes, interests, unconscious conflicts, personality types, and so forth. For our purposes, let us just say that a psychological test tells us what kind of person someone is, which is another way of saying that we have some idea of how he or she will act and react under specific circumstances. The usual methods of administering psychological tests include asking questions that require factual answers, asking more open-ended questions, having the person draw things, associate to words, describe what they see in ink blots, make up stories to fit pictures, and so forth.

This book is based on a seldom-used psychological test developed in Europe in 1939, the Wartegg Drawing Completion Test. Alix Goldsmith made some changes in it before administering it to a distinguished list of "willing victims." The current test consists of six squares, each bearing a different graphic sign. The subjects were asked to complete the drawings in each square and then to label them. Afterward, they were told that each square represents an important aspect of their personal views (self, others, the couple, life, sexuality, imagination), and they were asked to make interpretive comments on their own performance. These drawings and comments were subsequently turned over to me with no identification other than the gender and age of each subject. Any identifying words or phrases that crept into their responses were blacked out before I received them—although in a few cases the occupation of the subject was not hard to guess (a musician, a magician, an amateur metaphysician).

I was chosen for this task because I am a psychologist with long experience in the practice and teaching of psychological testing and of psychotherapy. In a professional capacity, I would not, of course, even dream of describing people sight unseen and on the basis of their playful performance on a test that was chosen because it is easy to use and because it is amusing.

Even a professional psychologist, however, has a right to have fun as long as he or she and his or her audience know and understand the context.

In a serious context, when important decisions may be based on a test (how to treat a disease, whom to admit to a professional school, how to advertise a new detergent or ice-cream, which car to buy, etc.) the makers of the test provide and the users of the test know (or *should* know) two things about it: its *reliability* and its *validity.*

As an example, take the SATs, which are widely used by college admission offices. Just as you would want to know that your bathroom scale is not going to give you measurements three pounds apart if you weigh yourself twice in a row, colleges want to know that a student's SAT scores will be the same whether the student takes the test in the morning or in the afternoon, in Vermont or in Florida; they also want to know that the score will not change depending on who scores the test. Actually, some error always creeps in, and there are complicated mathematical techniques that tell us whether scores such as those of the SATs are sufficiently *reliable.*

The SATs are, indeed, highly reliable, and this reliability is necessary but not sufficient to make them good tests: we also need to know their *validity.* To determine *validity,* first we might pick a thousand students who have taken the SATs. Then we would have to agree to some way in which we can determine the degree of these students' success in college. We would apply further mathematical procedures, which give us the correlation between SAT scores and college success. This correlation, then, is a measure of the validity of the SATs as predictors of success in college.

In short, *reliability* tells us the degree to which we can trust the accuracy of our measurements, and *validity* tells us to what extent the test is a test of what it claims to be testing.

Yet, in a less scientific but much more prevalent sense, we are all psychologists and we are constantly giving and and taking psychological tests, because we are always making inferences about people from the way they sit and walk, from what they say and how they say it, and from what they do. Consciously or unconsciously, we decide the person chatting with us at a party is meek or arrogant, street smart or naive, in a good mood or depressed, contented or angry—and our impressions in part determine how we act with the other person.

Projective tests—of which this Wartegg Drawing Test is one—hold an ambiguous, somewhat cloudy, midpoint position between mathematically precise, highly reliable and valid scientific tests at one end and purely intuitive, unsystematic impressions at the other. When asked to take a projective test, the subject is given standardized material—in other words, the task is the same for everyone taking the test. However, unlike an arithmetic question or questions about the capital cities of different countries, these tasks are highly open-ended; they permit a wide range of possible responses. Examples are Rorschach's test, which requires the subject to say what a standard set of ink-blots looks like to him or her, or the Thematic Apperception Test, which calls for stories to fit a standard set of pictures.

This book is based on a projective test which was not formally evaluated. We are not making scientific claims, nor am I practicing psychology in supplying my commentary. Nevertheless, everything we do, and particularly what we do in response to open-ended conditions, reflects our personality. There is, therefore, much information here about a number of people who arouse much curiosity in all of us.

Here is your chance to satisfy some of your curiosity, to draw your own conclusions from their responses, and to compare your conclusions with mine. Remember, a pinch of salt tends to improve the taste of most food. Take the following with a grain of salt, and have fun.

Michel Radomisli, Ph.D.,
Clinical Associate Professor at
Cornell University Medical College—
New York Hospital, Payne Whitney Clinic

ABOUT THE TEST

1 Prepare a blank test. (You may photocopy the test on the facing page, but cover up the meaning given for each box.)

2 Ask the participant to draw the first thing that comes to mind in each square and to label each drawing.

3 The squares are designed to reveal the participant's psychological profile in these areas: one's self, others, couples, life, sexuality, and imagination.

4 Once the participant has completed the test, tell him or her what each square actually means. Have fun deciphering the test together. See what new things you can learn about the participant's personality.

ONESELF   OTHERS   A COUPLE

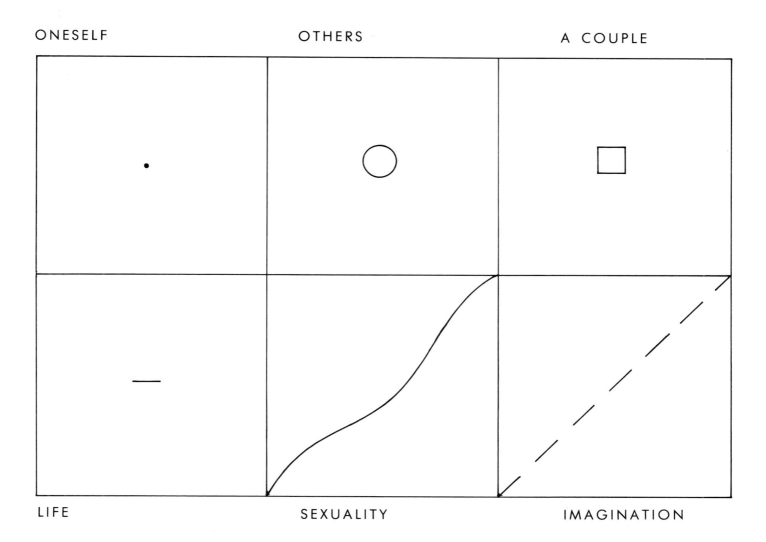

LIFE   SEXUALITY   IMAGINATION

ONESELF   OTHERS   A COUPLE

dots or stars

lightness

in or out

sitting

Flowing

over and under

LIFE   SEXUALITY   IMAGINATION

1 I see myself as a star.

2 Others are light, floating around.

3 "In or out" of relationship: very real, isn't it?

4 Life is like a bowl of cherries.

5 Flowing, essence, suggestion, liquid.

6 "Over and under." My imagination must be spatial. I think I have already come across this.

His pen exudes creativity. Look at the last square in the series: by the time he is through with it, it is almost impossible to see the original broken line, although none of it has been erased or blacked over. That transformation alone would testify to extraordinary visual creativity—and there is much more.

His words are few but to the point. He has a deservedly favorable view of himself, without a trace of arrogance. His self-esteem coexists with his affection and respect for others.

Experiencing inner harmony, he does not see himself in a struggle with others or with life: He can go with the flow. He's an artistic talent with an artistic attitude in tune with his environment, a happy man who makes those around him happy too.

DAVID HOCKNEY

PAINTER

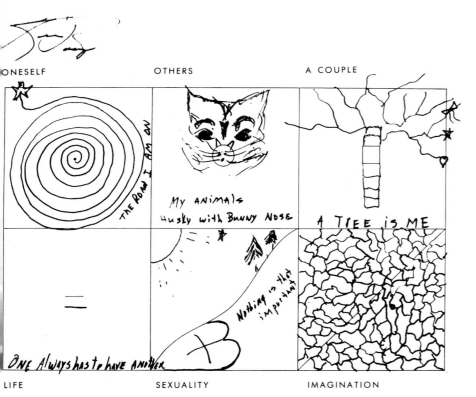

ONESELF   OTHERS   A COUPLE

THE ROAD I AM ON

MY ANIMALS
Husky with Bunny Nose

A TREE is ME

One Always has to have Another

Nothing is that important

LIFE   SEXUALITY   IMAGINATION

1 I always think I know where I'm going, but in fact I'm still learning and discovering where I am going. That's what makes life exciting, livable.

2 I love animals. I have a lot of animals, I drew my dog.

3 I love to see people who are happy together. There is so much pain and insecurity; it's too hard

to be alone. It's good to be able to share this pain and insecurity. Two happy people together is the most beautiful thing.

4 "One always has to have another." Again I repeat myself and unfortunately a lot of people don't agree. And so, it's nice to share the good and the bad, not to hide from the other—it's the greatest freedom.

5 I love sexuality. People don't use it enough. When you don't use it, you lose it! People are, unfortunately, ashamed or scared by it, though it's a gift, a game, a pleasure.

6 It's out of control! My head is about to burst open! It's everywhere!

▼ THE ANALYSIS

A vibrant, sensual woman, perhaps a touch too generous with her feelings, a touch too flamboyant for some tastes. She stresses, in this test, the importance of being in a couple to a degree that is puzzling. Was she at the height of an intense relationship? Was she at the time unattached and very much missing being part of a couple?

But why the emphasis on "this pain and insecurity" that are so good to share? I would think it is even better to share contentment, inner security, and joy.

Unsolicited advice: beware of relationships based on mutual "oh, you poor baby" feelings —they always turn sour, and if they don't, they survive at the cost of keeping both people down.

KIM BASINGER

ACTRESS

ONESELF   OTHERS   A COUPLE

2 wrongs don't make a right.

a Woody Allen Sci-Fi film.

Can you make the jump?

Butterfly's amazing

Franz Klammer — look out!

a pedestrian trying to cross the street

LIFE   SEXUALITY   IMAGINATION

1 I'm sorry, I only know how to answer specific questions. Oh my God. Well, I'm always afraid to doodle, because I always end up making phallic symbols. So when somebody now tells me, I make an effort to make circles, and I realize I got caught on this one. So . . . this is my best attempt. I guess that two wrongs don't make a right. A couple of phallic symbols heading off in different directions. The bad seed.

2 Well, now that I know that's what it is, I wish I could. I mean, I think Woody Allen has a pretty good attitude in respect of—about life. He points out the foibles and vulnerabilities of people without laughing at them, and always has a sense of social relationship, social intercourse. So, I would hope I would see other people in a way that I find humor without laughing at them, and would enjoy their company and at the same time realize they're not me. They could just as well be from another planet.

3 You say so—yeah. "You make the jump" —I think that's fairly self-explanatory. That must be the part of me there—that's supposed to be a hole, but I know where the bottom is. I think it's the right principle. I think it requires a large degree of risk and a certain amount of faith. But, I think it gets yourself through this life.

4 Well—I don't know. I guess that the butterflies were flying in the air and there was a lot of pollen, and they sneeze a little and that makes them go on. I guess in relation to that box, that life, and the question of the butterfly—and how beautiful it looks from the exterior only. Stays one day and dies the other.

And it's human, and there's a sense of humor.

If that box is life, life equals a sense of humor.

5 Well, Franz Klammer was, you know, the greatest downhill skier, greatest, the most dangerous, the one who took the most chances in his life as downhill skier, the one that I admire. So that's really going faster than Franz.

6 That's the guy stepping off the curb and those are the cars. The cars going by and finally he decides—he gives up. Well, imagination is really what

separates you from other forms of living beings. I mean, most—all mammals live and breathe and, you know, give birth and die, but humans are about the only ones who have an imagination. Maybe porpoises. So imagination's really important. Because it's the only thing that we have that kind of separates us from any species of animal.

They're very hard to—. I mean, it's one thing to have it interpreted by somebody else, but then you don't know what they are.

▼ THE ANALYSIS

Here we have the drawings of an imaginative, forceful man. His first comment, however, starts with "I'm sorry"— and this apology is typical of a personality trait which I think might weigh him down. Either he does not think of himself as successful, or he feels guilty because he believes he has acquired his success fraudulently.

"Two wrongs don't make a right," "The bad seed," "Stays one day and dies the other," "He gives up"—such pessimism! When he says things that reflect a sense of humor, a sense of compassion, a sense of proportion, he gives credit to someone else for these attributes. Well, Woody Allen may indeed have these qualities, but so does our subject. Why isn't he more sure of himself? Why does he see such a powerful barrier between himself and others?

He is, almost certainly, a fine man in addition to being a successful one—but he may walk around with a sense of it all being ephemeral, undeserved, precarious, as if there were a lien on his identity and the creditors might decide any moment to foreclose.

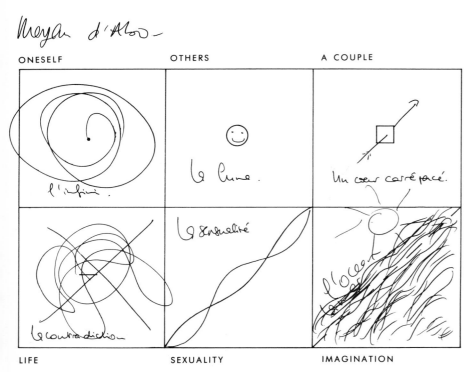

ONESELF · OTHERS · A COUPLE

l'infini.

le lune.

Un cœur carré percé.

le sensualité

le contradiction

LIFE · SEXUALITY · IMAGINATION

1 "The infinite." This little point is me, and I am tiny, tiny, tiny in the middle of this infinite, gigantic universe and I am just a little point. That's often how I feel.

2 "The moon." How do I see the others? I usually am quite positive about seeing others, but I love the moon. And there is an interpretation if you like the moon or not, and I do. And when I saw that, I thought of the film *Moonstruck*, the old man sitting on a bench, looking at the moon. It's the Mediterranean side in me.

3 I saw this square and I thought, you know, of *"Le coeur percé"* [the pierced heart] and I thought, there are square hearts. I don't know, it's the *côte perçant* [betrayal] in relation with people.

The corners of a heart.

4 "Contradiction." Well I saw this line and I hate lines. I love round shapes, sensuality, so I did it in contradiction and then I crossed it, because I always contradict myself, each time!

5 "Sensuality." I tried to follow the flow of it. It could also be a river, and this I did it as I saw the world upside down. There is a bump, like in a boat on the big ocean.

6 "Ocean, the sea." There are reflections, silver ones, like this. It's calm but it's overpowering and that's what I want to bring out. Overpowering ocean and nature overpowers you. There is the huge ocean, and you are so tiny next to it.

▼ THE ANALYSIS

The quintessential ingenue! The kind of young woman who repeatedly tells you (particularly if you are male) how tiny, how helpless she is in this difficult and dangerous and cruel world, by implication making you feel (particularly if you are male) big and strong and protective—and you want to put your big strong arms around her and protect her from all the meanies out there. It helps a great deal that when you put your arms around her you encounter not sharp elbows and scuffed knees but smooth, firm curves that provide a perfect fit and make you feel even better than you make *her* feel.

It's a great strategy with which to go through life, if you can do it. I suspect our subject does very well and is in fact much stronger than she appears and gives herself credit for.

MARYAM D'ABO

ACTRESS

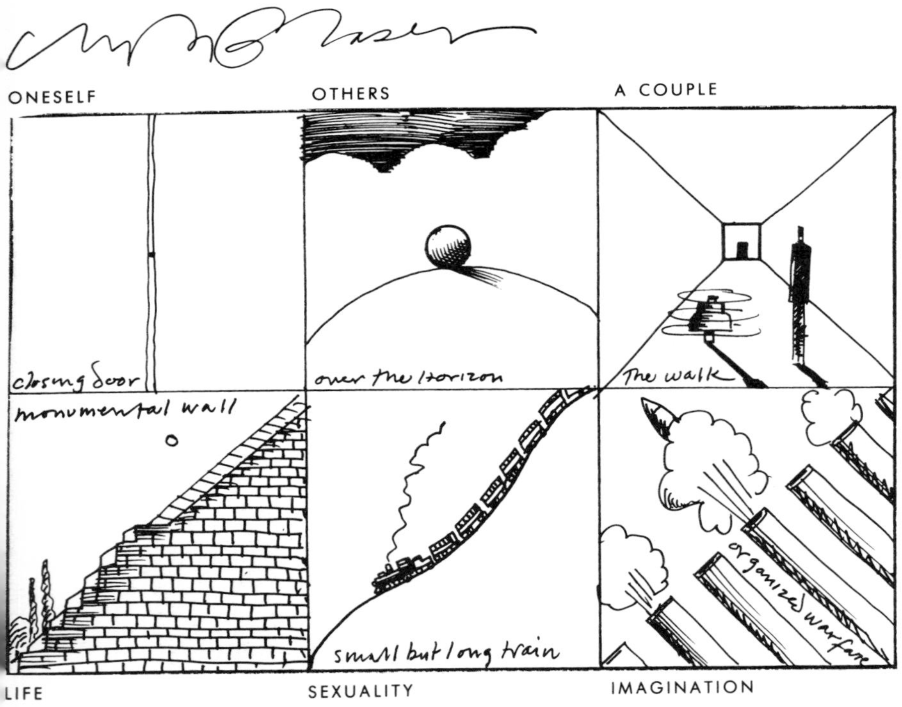

ONESELF   OTHERS   A COUPLE

closing door
monumental wall
over the horizon
The walk
small but long train
organized warfare

LIFE   SEXUALITY   IMAGINATION

1 Awareness and alienation.

2 Impossibility of knowing another.

3 Totally incompatible, going into a mad frenzy, yin and yang.

4 Life—a barrier which has to be transgressed, but luckily steps are here to help us get beyond. But it ain't easy.

5 The fact is that sex is not the center issue of my life in terms of being the driving force, but nevertheless it persists as being.

6 Reality thinks that imagination is a disorganized warfare because it's subversive.

▼ THE ANALYSIS

Hard to know, from this test performance, whether the subject is an artist, a philosopher, or a scientist. Since at their best, philosophers and scientists are also artists, whatever his concrete activity, he is an artist in any case.

His drawings are examples of exceptional creativity: he uses the given elements in very unusual ways while integrating them perfectly with the final product. His comments, brief as they are, reconcile the concepts attributed to each design with his drawings so ingeniously that the psychologist in me abdicates and falls silent with awe as I once more marvel at the spark given to a lucky few— and I am grateful for the ability to appreciate what they produce.

All art comes from the artist's self, of course; but the more successful the artistic transformation, the more opaque it is to the artist's personal needs, wishes, and fears. In spite of the obvious ease with which it was tossed off, this test performance qualifies as art, and I am reluctant to risk spurious interpretations based on it.

M I L T O N   G L A S E R

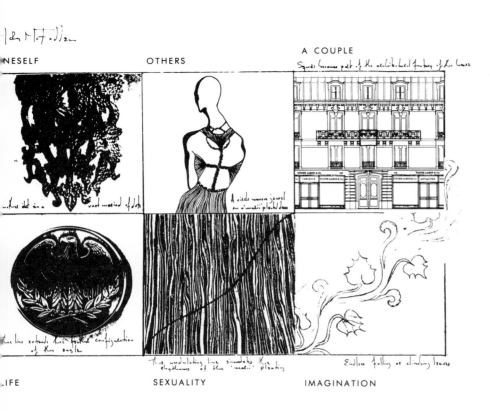

ONESELF
OTHERS
A COUPLE
LIFE
SEXUALITY
IMAGINATION

tasy of the house—squares are the double sides of the perfectly matched sides of the French windows. The French, architecturally, are perfect in drawing.

4 The line has become part of the feather configuration and extends the feather configuration of the eagle. It's a line. Seeing my life on the line being now, the past and future.

5 The undulating line simulates the rhythms of the moiré pleating. Sensuality of the fabric is to me the most romantic and ancient way of dressing—Egyptians, Ancient Greek or Chinese 450 B.C.–2000 B.C. Nothing is as beautiful as the original classical materials.

6 I took out the broken line—or filled it in. I didn't like that at all. I chose an endless line of leaves. It may be descending or ascending—letting it go out of page freely proves that imagination is limitless.

1 I'm putting a dot into hundreds of dots—pendants in a vast myriad.

2 Circle woven jewel on a moiré pleated dress. I'm always dressing people, embellishing them, making them as beautiful as I have the power to. The circle represents a disk that I often reproduce in my work—astrology circle—no beginning and no end.

3 The square becomes part of an architectural fan-

▼ THE ANALYSIS

A woman absolutely remarkable for exceptional talent, creativity, industry, and generosity of spirit.

You don't have to be a psychologist to see her eye for design and her skill in translating her vision into a product, and the fusion of artistry with craftsmanship. Her attention to detail, her absorption in every aspect of her production, her pride in her work and the pleasure she takes in it all suggest that she is among the lucky few whose identity and whose work are combined in a seamless whole.

Her generosity of spirit finds a wonderful outlet in her work: she genuinely enjoys sharing her creations, and not only for the financial rewards.

Perhaps not much time and place in her life for romance. Disappointed more than once? Exploited? Hurt? Disillusioned?

MARY MCFADDEN

FASHION DESIGNER

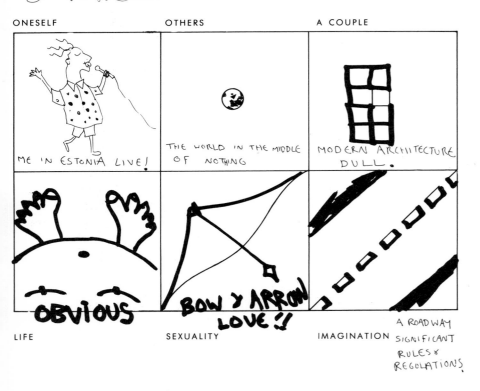

ONESELF OTHERS A COUPLE

ME IN ESTONIA LIVE!

THE WORLD IN THE MIDDLE OF NOTHING

MODERN ARCHITECTURE DULL.

OBVIOUS

BOW & ARROW LOVE!!

A ROADWAY SIGNIFICANT RULES & REGULATIONS

LIFE SEXUALITY IMAGINATION

1 I'm a pretty hilarious person then aren't I. Well, I got myself dead right.

2 If there is anything in space, it has yet to reveal itself. The human race currently is too stupid to realize, so nothing it is.

3 I would not say that squares represent couples at all. Quite the opposite, I would say the circles do. All straight lines end up as circles anyway.

4 That's just a curve of a stomach. That's what I see every day when I wake up! Oh God another day!

5 Got that one, didn't I!

6 Oh well, I could have done better.

▼ THE ANALYSIS

He says he is "a pretty hilarious person"—and maybe he is. In the test, though, what shows up is not hilarity as much as pugnacity. Just as some people automatically joke in response to things, our subject tends to be automatically argumentative, to maintain the opposite of most propositions.

I can't quite see why he has to spend so much energy in presenting himself as a rebel. Perhaps his upbringing was oppressive, and being a rebel was the road to psychological survival. Perhaps, in spite of his success (or even because of his success), he feels his position to be tenuous, and he has to act tough to preempt expected assaults from others.

A little less of a biting edge to his humor, a little more tolerance for the "currently too stupid" human race, a little more respect for himself and for others—all of that would go a long way to make him and those around him feel better.

JOHNNY ROTTEN

MUSICIAN, THE SEX PISTOLS

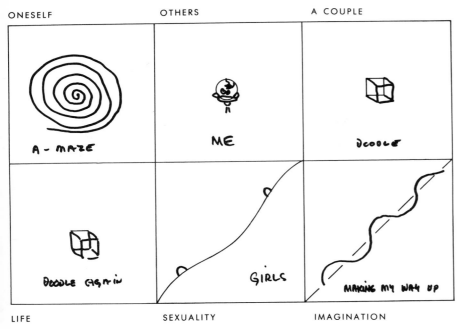

ONESELF   OTHERS   A COUPLE

A - MAZE   ME   DOODLE

DOODLE AGAIN   GIRLS   MAKING MY WAY UP

LIFE   SEXUALITY   IMAGINATION

3 All boxed in, I guess. Guess that's what that is. I guess doing a box is a confined sort of feeling rather than doing people who do these kind of things. I don't know whether it means protection or whether it would mean that I feel confined or boxed in by a couple. I think that I am pretty much an individual that wants to do it alone, rather than as a partnership with someone.

4 Well, I'm doing again the boxed-in feeling with life. I guess maybe I feel confined by my life, possibly.

5 I've always liked girls. When I was a child, when I was a kid in school I used to draw girls. This, I didn't know what to do.

6 Well, I think imagination is important for me. I imagine all the time. I daydream some, which I guess most people do. I imagine myself in different situations. I imagine where I'm going to be. I like to travel, so I probably imagine myself moving a lot. I do move around a lot. I was thinking more in terms of wending my way. I've traveled. And hoping to end up, you know, that's why I said "up", I guess. Well, it is up. I guess you could look at it being flat, or looking down, but I'd rather look at it as being up. Okay! Did I pass?

▼ T H E   A N A L Y S I S

A competent, sensible, unpretentious,

successful man whose modesty approaches

1 Going in circles, I guess, and it can also be a tunnel, but it is "a maze." Or also the other way, "amaze." Must be the way I go through life, you know, finding my way probably going in circles.

2 I guess I think that people are funny. Or childish. Or young, always. It's nice to be childish, we have to keep that.

self-denigration. Perhaps he is not a once-in-a-generation genius, but he is the kind of person who is essential to the success of projects dreamt up by visionaries. He refuses to take himself seriously and is a reliable companion and co-worker, but he underestimates himself to the point of perplexing those around him—they respect him more than he respects himself.

He is wary of excess emotionality and cannot tolerate histrionics either in himself or in others. He can come across as cold and unfeeling, although much of his aloofness is directly due to a remnant of shyness basic to his character.

A loner in some ways, self-sufficient and self-reliant. In a distant nook of his personality, he nurtures a dream of breaking through barriers, of liberation, of an explosion and transformation that will give him access to qualities and intensities of yet untasted experience and emotion.

ANDY WILLIAMS

SINGER

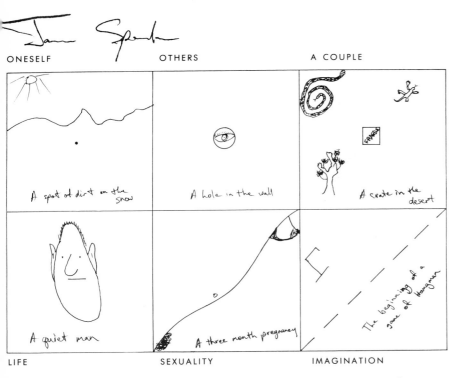

ONESELF   OTHERS   A COUPLE

A spot of dirt on the snow

A hole in the wall

A crate in the desert

A quiet man

A three month pregnancy

The beginning of a game of Hangman

LIFE   SEXUALITY   IMAGINATION

1 All right, "a spot of dirt on the snow." Yeah, that's me, a spot of dirt on the snow. That sounds good. I've really gotten into something here. Well, I don't know, it should have been piss on the snow or something. No, it isn't that. I shouldn't have said that. A spot of dirt on the snow. Oh, God, go on to the next one, that's too difficult.

2 How I see others? "A hole in the wall." Well, you know, to be honest with you, I can't see the connection between any of these and what they're supposed to represent. Either they are looking at me or I am looking at them through a little hole, I guess that's it.

3 I can't see the connection between that and couples at all, except you did point out the tree and the snake, but the lizard's in there and so's a crate. So, what does that mean? I don't know.

4 A quiet man's life. Well, that seems sort of appropriate though, you know, life is; no, it's not! There's no connection between that and life, really, is there? Except, maybe, a quiet man sort of learns more about life than all those people out there that are making a lot of noise, you know? Maybe, that's true. Maybe people who have more answers when they die are the people who haven't spent all their time yapping away.

5 The sexuality thing, a three-month pregnancy? Christ, well, I drew the tit too small, and the stomach is huge, you know, compared to the tit, but maybe that's because I've got babies on my mind (my wife is pregnant), so maybe that has to do with my sexuality right now.

6 And this one, imagination, "the beginning of a game of hangman." I don't know, that sort of looks like sort of cop-out, doesn't it? Well, how many letters do we have here? One, two, three, four, five, six, seven. Seven letters. What's a good seven-letter word that has to do with imagination? I don't know if I can get one so quickly with a tape recorder in front of me.

A time of turbulence. Very much in the public eye, but the satisfaction of fame and success could be marred by feelings of inadequacy. In the midst of plenty, he sometimes sees himself in a desert, unable to take advantage of the goodies provided by life. Perhaps he is asking himself whether a quiet life away from glitter is not preferable after all.

He could be trying to come to terms with the thought of himself as a family man, as a father. All in all, there seems to be a pervasive sense here of some difficulty in experiencing pleasure and joy—perhaps he is depressed. He is making an effort to come across as assertive, as rough and tough, but his distress is breaking through anyway.

Is all this a stable aspect of his personality, or did the test catch him at a bad time?

J A M E S   S P A D E R

A C T O R

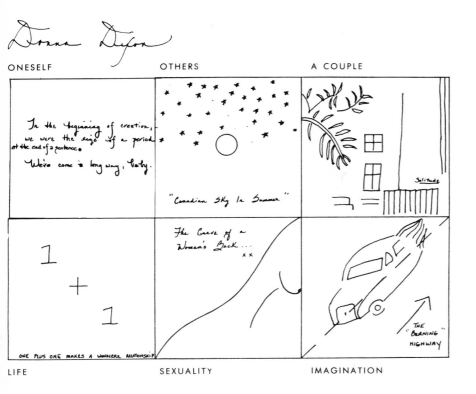

ONESELF   OTHERS   A COUPLE

In the beginning of creation, we were the size of a period at the end of a sentence.
We've come a long way, baby.

"Canadian Sky In Summer"

Solitude

1
+
1

The Curve of a Woman's Back...
x x

THE "BURNING" HIGHWAY

ONE PLUS ONE MAKES A WONDERFUL RELATIONSHIP

LIFE   SEXUALITY   IMAGINATION

1 When I saw the dot, I didn't think about myself, but the child that was growing inside of me.

2 I picture myself lying in a field in a back of a pickup truck, looking up into the star-filled summer sky of Canada. If the circle represents others, then the moon is myself; I am the center of my universe and the stars are my loved ones—all of my bright lights in my life. I love them close and yet far enough so they can have their own independence and freedom of self-expression.

3 Well, I pictured home. Solitude and peacefulness, and that's what the best relationship should always bring. Nice. . . . That's life.

4 "1+1=2" Two independent souls coming together in love, *forever*. Because you see, my friend, one plus one will *always* equal two, *forever*.

5 The beautiful body of a woman . . . need I say more?

6 Imagination? Yeah, on fire. Roaring. Speeding to its destination. Onward to exploration, to self-discovery. Life after thirty.

▼ T H E   A N A L Y S I S

A woman who is bubbling with self-satisfaction and overflowing with love—a

46

fine example of the synergy between self-esteem and openness to strong loving relations with others, without absorbing them or being absorbed by them.

She is as concerned with physical attractiveness as any woman is, if not more so. Yet, unlike many women, she sees the passage of time as an opportunity for discovery: time to her is not an adversary but an ally. She does not anticipate the future years with dread, because she knows that every age, every phase in life can be beautiful in its own way.

An intelligent, sensitive woman, probably happily married.

DONNA DIXON

Jon Lovitz

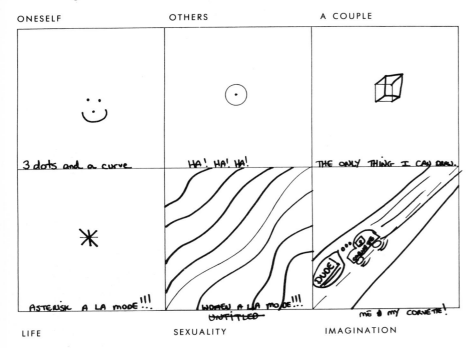

ONESELF · OTHERS · A COUPLE

3 dots and a curve

HA! HA! HA!

THE ONLY THING I CAN DRAW.

ASTERISK A LA MODE...!!!

WOMEN A LA MODE...!!!
~~UNTITLED~~

DUDE

me & my CORVETTE!

LIFE · SEXUALITY · IMAGINATION

1 I've got more hair than this! That's sure.

2 Seems funny to me!

  As I must seem funny to them.

3 This means that they are always changing, I'm guessing.

4 Happiness plus dessert!

  Dessert is very important. I never share my dessert or my women. The most important: *joie de vivre!* Like the star, make the most out of it.

5 I love women, curves, shapes, sensations, like a guitar—I really do love women. Women and dessert! Best things in life. Though desserts are more sure!

6 *Freedom!*

  Imagination is what I want it to be. And in that car!

This man uses whimsy as a way of hiding, as a ploy to remain unrelated and disconnected—and the camouflage works. I have no idea about what kind of person he is, what makes him tick. His drawings hardly go beyond little jokes, and the only thing he says he can draw is a cube whose perceptual ambiguity keeps you suspended in uncertainty. (Which is the front plane? Are you sure? Keep looking and wait for the shift.)

One would think that "I love women" and "I love dessert" are at least clear statements —but when you love "women" rather than *a* woman, when women are "curves, shapes, sensations, like a guitar," and when desserts are seen as more reliable than women, how much love can you expect for a specific person?

My point is not that he is incapable of loving or that he puts women on a par with chocolate cake; my point is that *I* am incapable of saying anything about him that you can sink your teeth into.

JON LOVITZ

ACTOR

Mick Jones

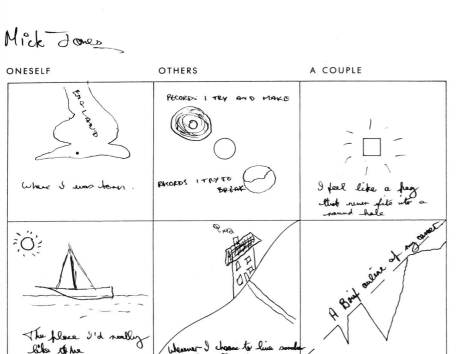

ONESELF — England. Where I was born.

OTHERS — RECORDS I TRY AND MAKE. RECORDS I TRY TO BREAK.

A COUPLE — I feel like a peg that never fits into a round hole.

LIFE — The place I'd really like to be.

SEXUALITY — Wherever I choose to live something looks like this.

IMAGINATION — A Brief outline of my career.

1 How I see myself? I guess that means that my heart is where I was born, where maybe I'll go back. I saw a picture the other day of an English sky, with two white clouds, Yeah, I probably will go back.

2 That's interesting, "records." I don't know what that means, what I've done there. At the moment, I'm trying to make a record and break up the band that I was working with. This is funny, because now I'm working with a bunch of other people. I'm with a new group. It's another production I'm doing.

3 A peg, like a square peg which doesn't fit into the round hole, I'm not sure if it's a square peg actually; in other words, something that doesn't fit into things.

4 That speaks for itself, doesn't it? This is my dream, I mean, I really would like to spend my life like that. At least, part of my life like that.

5 I had to put a bikini on it. Sexuality with my little house. No, it represents a sort of slope like that which never feels like it's quite stable.

6 This is the line of my life, career, its ups and downs and wherever it's going now. It took a little surge there. It's funny.

Here we have a competent, successful person, probably doing what he is best equipped to do, living a life he is best suited for—and he claims that he would rather live elsewhere, that he would rather do something else, and that he feels like a square peg trying to squeeze into a round hole. I am sure, incidentally, that he is absolutely sincere in these claims, that he fully believes them himself. He is, therefore, among those people who do very well, are often envied by others for their talent and for their accomplishments, but who live their lives with a feeling of tentativeness, of temporariness, of waiting for things to be different so they can do what they *really* want to do. Ironically, it is precisely this feeling of dissonance that energizes them, that provides them with the incentive to work hard in preparation for the life they supposedly *really* want to live. Put this man in a country house in England with access to a sailboat under two white clouds, and he probably wouldn't know what to do with himself. He would soon be on the phone, talking to people in London, in New York, in L.A., and planning deals.

When he reads this, he will decide I am wrong and will continue to work hard, dreaming of retiring in Sussex or Essex or wherever.

MICK JONES

MUSICIAN, FOREIGNER

Catherine Oxenberg

ONESELF	OTHERS	A COUPLE
seeing the truth	Radiance	Light at the end of the tunnel
Intuitive	Waves and vibration	upward propelling path

| LIFE | SEXUALITY | IMAGINATION |

1 Okay, are we on? I think this would very much describe who I am as a person and my spiritual past, which is, I'm a seeker. A seeker—it's not someone who wears a white turban around their head. It's somebody who searches and is somebody who's unbelievably curious about life and is looking for the answers, and who is completely open to all reality. I'm extremely receptive, and I never prejudice myself by closing out possibilities until they feel right in my heart. So, it's definitely higher.

2 Others? I always look for the beauty in people and that makes me very idealistic. And also sometimes I'm disappointed because what I see is I see straight through to the core of the beauty of a person, and then sometimes whatever idiosyncrasies, whatever they project in terms of as idiosyncrasies may not be so high, in terms of petty characteristics, sometimes let me down because I tend to just see—. No, let me put it in a better way. I'm unconventional. Most people, when they meet somebody, they're limited by preconceptions, the idea you have of someone. Especially if they're well known. People project what they want of themselves, and I tend to see the inner and simple beauty about people so that's definitely true.

3 Well, I didn't know that I was so idealistic. I think that's lovely that I think that marriage for me will be such a wonderful path, such a balance. (You're not going to take a picture of me today. I'll kill you.)

I think that's lovely. I think that means that everything I believe about finding one's soulmate and to be a perfect partner in life and a perfect balance is also my deepest belief, and I'm happy with that.

4 Hmm . . . It's very interesting that I should put a cartoon cat with "intuitive."

My life?

Again big eyes . . . Well what I love about cats is the fact that they are so intuitive, that we should use them as familiars because they're psychic animals and that they have such a perfect integration of body, in terms of balance and grace. They epit-

omize balance and grace for me. So for me to develop my intuitive side as opposed to just my mental intellective would be the core of balance and harmony in my life.

5 Sexuality? I can't, I don't know what to make out of this one. Yeah, vibrant, confidently strong, no?

Well, it shows a lot of rhythm and movement in it, doesn't it? There's a great deal of energy about it, untapped energy I would say. And rhythm and radiance . . . well again there's radiance in there. It's lovely and very subtle and very graceful. Yeah, I would say there's a lot of sexual energy but it seems like it can be transmitted, it's just pure energy. The body . . . the body of water is perfect.

6 This is my imagination? I have a wonderful imagination and very inspiring and also with a great deal of lofty thoughts. So my imagination? Well, I believe that the only limitations in life are your fears, so that whatever you can perceive or imagine you can create as a reality. So, I know that for me the way I see life in an idealistic sense is that we are meant to break boundaries, so that's freedom. So this for me shows my imagination leading

me to freedom and guiding me outwards to some sort of self-realization. Self accounts now. Inner self—not self with a big ego. Yeah. Because a lot of people with whom I'll talk about the self get very caught up in semantics about what that represents. To me the self is always with a little s, meaning it's how it flows with the rest of the universe. I mean that we're all the same "self." But I like that, because it's not wasting any time. There's no deviation, it's just going straight upwards.

Perfect. So it's done!

▼ THE ANALYSIS

A talented, sensitive, gentle, and well-meaning young woman. But good will is not enough.

Her "openness to reality," her tolerance, her "idealism" have a heavy component of condescension, of narcissistic superiority—

and I am sure she would be hurt to hear this because at heart she is a kind and decent person. But there is a naivete about her that makes her trust her intuition and intellect implicitly and without reservation. Yet she is too young to be wise and has not worked hard enough and long enough at honing her intellect.

Wisdom does not come cheaply. Intuition has to be tested repeatedly and has to be tempered with skepticism. Intellect requires much patient and sometimes tedious work toward accumulation of technique, of information, of knowledge. With true humility, time, and hard academic work her internal self may come closer to the perfection which she seems to be already attributing to it.

In the meantime, she is a very pleasant person—but perhaps a trifle spoiled.

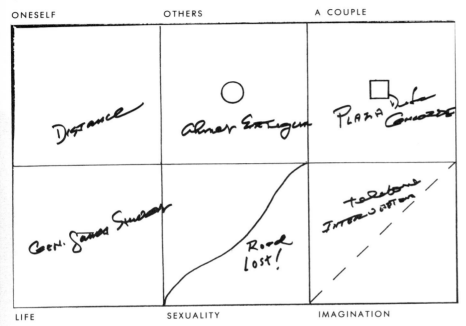

Jocelyn P. Lester

ONESELF	OTHERS	A COUPLE
Distance	⚪ Ahmet Ertegun	⬜ PLAZA Vista Commozze
Gen. James Steward	Road Lost!	telephone Interruption
LIFE	SEXUALITY	IMAGINATION

1 Long distance.

Even though I'm 80 years old, I don't feel as if life is closing in on me at all. Life is action and doing things. I have plans to travel, people to see, people who are amusing. That's what life's about for me. I'm looking forward to going to China. I'm looking forward to Venice this summer.

2 Ahmet Ertegun, a man I admire very much, has a great zest for life; this is also true of his wife.

They are both great givers. Very generous, always ready to find new adventures, happenings, and when they can't get you to do it, they do it, and they are very gifted in making their life an adventure. I admire generosity in all my friends. I cannot tolerate people who are stingy, cowardly. Ahmet and Mica Ertegun are the personification of people who are very gifted and generous.

3 I know very few people who are ecstatic about their marriages. Most people are probably cynical about it. You get attached to somebody, feel very strongly about that person on many levels besides sexuality.

I think that's what love is all about. Divorce is when you lose all sense of friendship and respect—when you no longer respect the other.

6 I think people who are very successful are generally people with great imagination. They are successful because they visualize events. I think people should let their imagination guide their way of life, the place where they want to live, with whom and what they want to accomplish, and once they do that—to persue it, to try to catch the rainbow. It's not difficult; it depends on how you set your sights. Some people may set their objectives too high, so that their imagination gets the better of their judgment, and they fail because they haven't evaluated their ability to cope with what they've set out to do. On the other hand, overreaching is not too bad.

A level of energy, of vitality, of life-force that would be the envy of most people half his age. His very clearly stated stance is action-oriented, extraverted, emphatic about the importance of relationships, or friendships, or enduring bonds.

His strength is also his weakness. His world, in order to function smoothly, relies on interdependence, on personal favors and good will, and on admiration to the point of hero worship. This could result in restlessness when he is thrown solely upon his own resources; it could also make him vulnerable to disappointment.

The personality of a facilitator, of an expert, of an art dealer rather than of an artist—and of a successful example of his field. A superb catalyst who brings out the best efforts of those around him.

IRVING (SWIFTY) LAZAR

AGENT

ONESELF OTHERS A COUPLE

LIFE SEXUALITY IMAGINATION

1 I saw millions of dots. The dot is from a dream reoccurring, flying dreams in which I always lose the power of being able to fly, because I come back to earth and try to teach everyone else to fly. In this drawing everybody else learns to fly, and I can keep flying too!

2 I had a broken leg and have just spent eight months in bed, so this does make sense. There is a hospital bed, the eye is on the bed with a fishing pole, fishing in the rain with clocks set at different times. Sun rays are coming out of the eye. The fishing pole is made out of bamboo, something I used a lot as a child, the cork bobbin diving into the puddle at the foot of the bed. I don't

▼ THE ANALYSIS

An unusually imaginative woman who is generous with her talent, and energetic, and productive. Also, she is very aware of being gifted. Unlike many gifted people who derive pleasure from their sense of superiority, this woman's pleasure comes from sharing her gift with others, from wanting to bestow some of it on others so they can also taste the same joys.

She is also very introspective and very attentive to her inner life. Again, instead of the obsessive self-scrutiny this trait often leads to, for her it becomes a source of her art and therefore something to be shared in comprehensible form.

Her concern for the need to unify the planet whose residents we all are, her concern for the resources of the planet, are admirable. But why, oh why, are women seen as earth's potential saviors, while men are the bad guys of her global scenario?

know what I'm fishing, maybe ghost selves that I fish out at different times.

3 It's an open box with two of us in it. It has its side and top. It can also be shut if necessary. First, I had it floating in the ocean, then I built a rock, then I turned it into a cliff which rose out of the sea with a palm tree for shade. Solid ground, but you can get plunked by a coconut.

4 Religious symbols keeping sister moon and brother sun apart. Men are short-term, linear thinkers: hunters (bring the antelope down now!). And women are long-term circular thinkers (how do we feed the kids for the next years?), caretakers. Our brains are physically different, obviously to protect and grow with each other, to be in balance together.

After three thousand years or so of monotheistic patriarchy, or hunter "catch it, kill it, use it now" thinking in charge of the planet, and the caretaking female reins rusting in the closet of Judeo-Christianity—or Dungeon of Islam—we have almost run out of those long-term necessities like breathable air, clean water, land, and ozone envelope. We've been human for 30,000? 50,000 years or so and in only 3,000 years of an unbalanced idea, we've almost called it a day.

5 Ah, well, no wonder! It's my favorite children's story (other than the Brothers Grimm) about a small caboose that couldn't get up the hill by itself but keeps trying and finally with a little help—from its friends—makes it! Perseverence furthers.

6 First I saw a road, then a bridge, then being a woman, I sunk it in concrete and steel.

Nietszche's quote:

"Man is a rope tied between beasts and overmen —A rope over an abyss." A dangerous across, a dangerous on-the-way, a dangerous looking back, a dangerous shuddering and stopping. What is great in man is that he is a bridge and not an end: What can be loved in a man is that he is an overture and a going under.

LAUREN HUTTON

ACTRESS/MODEL

Armand Hammer

ONESELF	OTHERS	A COUPLE
(handwritten) I think the summit in Moscow, on May 29 & June 2 1988 will be a great success.	*(handwritten)* I hope Gorbachev and Reagan will agree to a 90% reduction in strategic weapons	*(handwritten)* I hope they will agree to do away with all chemical weapons

LIFE	SEXUALITY	IMAGINATION
(handwritten) I hope M.G. and R.R. agree to increase the emigration of Jews from the USSR	*(handwritten)* I hope M.G.R. R.R. agree to "scrap" Jackson-Vanik amendment for 5 yrs and agree to give the U.S.S.R. M.F.N.	*(handwritten)* I hope the two leaders agree to another summit in Washington before the end of the year and future President continue the policies of gradually eliminate all nuclear weapons...

1 I think the summit in Moscow on May 29th to June 2nd 1988 will be a great success.

2 I hope Gorbachev and Reagan will agree to a 50 percent reduction in strategic weapons.

3 I hope they will agree to do away with all chemical weapons.

4 I hope Mikhail Gorbachev and Ronald Reagan agree to increase the emigration of Jews from the U.S.S.R.

5 I hope M.G. and R.R. agree to scrap the Jackson-Vannick amendment for five years and agree to give the U.S.S.R. Most Favored Nation trade status.

6 I hope the two leaders agree to another summit in Washington before the end of the year, and future presidents continue the process of gradually eliminating all nuclear weapons and the reduction of conventional weapons.

▼ T H E   A N A L Y S I S

Because this man's drawings and comments were so limited, not much can be said about the kind of person he was. Still, in this collection of unusually interesting people, he was one of the most interesting.

His hand had a slight tremor, and his eyesight probably wasn't what it used to be, yet in his nineties he was younger than most men and women half his age: he was passionately interested in things and was well-informed in his areas of interest—he was not just echoing received ideas from yesterday's headlines. Furthermore, his main concern was with peace and disarmament—with an ideal toward which he could not expect to see much progress in his lifetime. He was deeply rooted in the history as well as the future of the planet and of the species; he was a true citizen and his global loyalty and identification put him at one with our world in the most fundamental sense possible. Louis XIV is reputed to have said "Après moi le déluge"; our subject was at the most admirably opposite pole of that attitude. No doubt he had attracted criticism for being unrealistically utopian, for being a deluded visionary, perhaps even for being a subversive influence: but this is criticism which has always been directed against those ahead of their times.

ARMAND HAMMER

Malcolm Forbes [signature]

ONESELF: A dot precedes an important paragraph when I'm writing editorials

OTHERS: For those in their right minds, the sun always shines — even behind the clouds

A COUPLE: a painting by Josef Albers

LIFE: Nothing and no one's ever flat ever

SEXUALITY: A chart projecting America's future / NOW

IMAGINATION: a chart of what news happens to corporate profits

1 This is myself. Well, I don't think that there are any stops to my own life until it is over, and I don't quite know what significance the point has, but being a writer, I think of it in terms of representing a period, as in a sentence structure. As far as my life is concerned, I don't like it to be full of periods. I like it to keep flowing. Okay. Next!

2 Others. This circle is supposed to represent others? Well. For those in their right mind. Listen, without others. . . . Ahahah. We would not be—there would be no life. Others are of all consequence to anyone, as anything could be. There has to be a relation. Okay. Next?

3 What do I think of couples? I think coupling is fun. Couples in general. Again, it takes two to tango. There is no life without a couple. So I don't think everything has to come in pairs but I think pairing off is great fun.

4 Well, I certainly do not see my life as flat, as I wrote here. Spell that word: "nothing and no one is ever flat." So I don't see my life as being on an even keel.

5 Big circles. I think having the line up is better.

I think the education here is that, you know . . . it goes on . . . it's a never ending story. It's an upbeat thing. Is that all right? It's a line going up!

6 Imagination. Most important of all. Well, I don't think of a broken line in relation to imagination. There are no such things as broken lines. I don't see the connection, but I am not a psychologist.

I think there is no success without imagination; there is no creativity without imagination. Everything to anyone whose motor runs, anything can set off the imagination, whether it's literature, or music, or art. Imagination is a vital ingredient of a full, exciting, and meaningful life. The worst condemnation that you can say of somebody, quite aside from obvious things—you know, evil or whatnot—I think the worst condemnation is that they have no imagination. What you mean is they're dead but not interred. Imagination is really the sparkplug or the petrol of life.

Here's a man whose driving ambition was to be larger than life, and he did not seem displeased with his achievement. Like many talented and successful men, he was egocentric and was capable of seeing other people as instruments of his power in all spheres— professional, personal, sexual. His actions were important to him by definition, simply because they were *his* actions. His narcissism was made tolerable by the fact that he *was,* in fact, a man of imagination and of effective action.

The fly in the ointment? The difficulty he had reconciling himself to the waning of physical and mental vitality that comes with aging. He did not welcome the quiet wisdom and placidity others associate with getting older. Just as some find solace in religion and others in the perpetuation of family, our subject found solace in the idea of "America." He was a patriot and his patriotic optimism was, at least in part, related to his vision of immortality through the survival and progress of his country.

M A L C O L M   F O R B E S

P U B L I S H E R

ONESELF	OTHERS	A COUPLE
HAPPY +SAD	SUN	House
TRAPEZE	SKIING	HAIL BRITANNIA
LIFE	SEXUALITY	IMAGINATION

1 Joy and gloom.

2 Sun in the morning.

3 Symbolic of family.

4 Life trapeze—amusement.

5 I own Aspen!

6 Britannia represents history.

▼ THE ANALYSIS

A successful, confident man, sure of his place in the sun. But a very sparse test record. Not much drawing, and even less speech. Yet this is not the product of a shy, retiring, taciturn man. Therefore (and because he is included in this book), I can rule out the possibility of our having a rather simple person here.

The alternative explanation is that the test did not engage him deeply, that his response was perfunctory.

MARVIN DAVIS

BUSINESSMAN

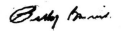

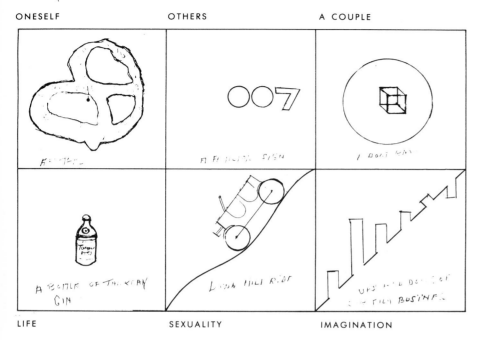

ONESELF   OTHERS   A COUPLE

LIFE   SEXUALITY   IMAGINATION

1 **A pretzel.**

2 **A familiar sign.**

3 **I don't know.**

4 **A bottle of Tanqueray gin.**

5 **Downhill ride.**

6 **Ups and downs of our**

film business.

A solid, reliable, successful person. Sure of his stature, confident in his achievement. He has an imagination that does not necessarily soar to magical heights, but which nevertheless can produce pleasing complexity, even with very little initial material.

The test may have caught him at one of his more vulnerable times: he seems worried about "going downhill." There just may be more inner turmoil in this man than is visible to the outsider. To the world at large, I repeat, he is a real solid citizen. If *he* had said more about his drawings, *I* could say more about him.

CUBBY BROCCOLI

PRODUCER/DIRECTOR

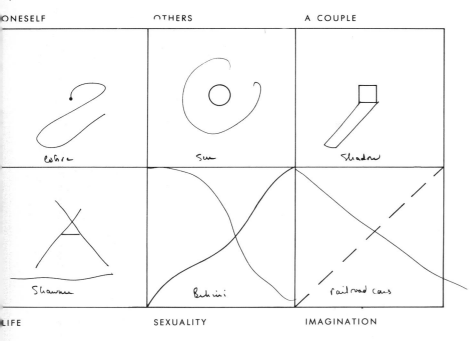

ONESELF   OTHERS   A COUPLE

Cobra   Sun   Shadow

Shawnee   Bikini   railroad cars

LIFE   SEXUALITY   IMAGINATION

1 I never thought of myself as a cobra!

2 If this is my evaluation of other people, it's quite clear that I enjoy them, if this is the sun.

3 I've drawn a picture of a shadow. I suppose it would mean that my relationships with others are ephemeral.

4 A tepee.

Life is difficult; it's like the Indians on the reservations—they don't have all that of a good time.

5 A bikini. That means I have an obsession with sex!

6 This is rather good because these are railway cars moving across as seen from above, seen from a crow's eye. So that would not cross most people's mind. So maybe that suggests that I'm doing what I should be doing to write. I should write more novels.

An intelligent, imaginative, versatile man whose forte is not in the graphic arts. His thinking, on the other hand, is remarkable for its flexibility, fluidity, fantasy.

His relationships with others tend to be friendly, warm, cordial, jovial—but without much intensity and complication. He has buddies, pals, chums rather than close friends.

Others enjoy his company more than *he* enjoys it. One function other people serve for him is that of distraction from a depressive tendency. Another very successful way in which he wards off unpleasant inner states is to take a distant, sometimes humorous perspective and to become a commentator on events rather than an initiator.

Listening to him and/or reading what he writes must be very pleasant.

G E O R G E   P L I M P T O N

W R I T E R / P U B L I S H E R

Dan
Aykroyd

ONESELF   OTHERS   A COUPLE

GALACTIC TRAVEL

SYMBOLS
SYMBOLOGY

PULL
OVER

RUNNING

CRYSTALS & MAGMA
H DIMENSIONAL
EXPLORATION

HUMAN
FACTOR

THE
ROAD

LIFE   SEXUALITY   IMAGINATION

1 Okay. Well, I think this one's—the first one's— right on, because I see myself as someone who's earthbound and wants to travel and soar into the nebulae. I love UFOs. Maybe I've seen two distant sightings, and I can pretty well say—. I had a vivid dream once and there was a sighting in upstate New York, and after I had the dream, we found out the next day that there was a sighting, and I had had the dream before there was the sighting. It was last June in New York state. And I love Carl Sagan's books, because he really laid it out.

Well, life is not only three dimensions as we see, we are just the pinpricks of what's below the surface, these little organisms, these *human* organisms we call ourselves. And there's so many more dimensions to life.

2 How I see others? Well, that applies I think, because I guess if you are a Jungian you can take the symbols and be pretty quickly involved in how symbols come at you. And, I suppose other people are the living representation of symbols. As far as the second one applying to how I see other people, well, I've got a lot of Jewish friends. Christian friends, and some Islamic friends. Well, I see, the circle represents a sort of an entity. It represents the world, it represents reality—it's a symbol of harmony, and it's a symbol of yin/yang which can be included in there, and it's also a symbol of all things coming back and coming around. And

that has to do with cosmology, and so, you know, I think of symbols.

3 This one's not on for me, running. Unless, I'm doing it with Donna, you know, I'm not doing it alone. I like to run away from situations having to do with work and stress and get away from the job. I usually do it with my spouse, you see. But sometimes, in a marriage, I suppose you can run from the responsibilities, and working on the marriage, it requires constant work. So, there is a little running, and you need time apart.

So, I'm sure people probably do run. But they run back to each other too, I hope. I think my wife is with me in the car and, if she is with me in the car, well, you see we're getting stopped!

4 This applies perfectly, doesn't it! Really, because crystals explode and they're so organic. Crystals and magma are organic. Have you ever seen those big hunks of metal magma? It looks like they're machined surfaces, you know—squared-off. And crystals too look like that. And they are perfectly designed, but they are too symmetrical to be designed by nature. Well, symmetry is throughout nature. And life and nature and symmetry are certainly all interlinked, and there're so many dimensions into life.

You see, you meet someone and there's one dimension and one face. And then, there're other facets. And then, he explodes like a tetrahedron. There're so many sides into people. So, crystals and magma are all organic, and you know, the eleventh plane is where we cross into parallel realities. Well, they think that the seventh plane is where the parallel reality—the good parallel reality—to earth might begin. I mean, some of the earths I've drawn here. I guess, I've drawn what any red-blooded North American kid would probably draw: UFOs, crystals, cop cars, religious symbols from I was raised as a Catholic, so, you know, the cross is in there.

5 And, "human factor"? Well, nice soft curves there, sexuality, human sexuality, yeah. I guess, this applies perfectly, because I saw a nice soft curve here and this looks like the curve of a woman's body, doesn't it? I put faces in here. The human factor surfaces! Those are hiding behind her, but don't let them get ideas. And they look like they either hate sex or they want real sex! But, I really think they want it!

6 Well, imagination. When I saw these lines, I immediately thought of a highway just following a road. And then, from that, what first idea popped

into my head was, you know, road, rodents, cactus, just that vast open desert and, I suppose, you could hook up the imagination. Kids are so lucky; they have the best imagination. So, I have to try and stay young, which I am—if you look at my drawings, very childish. Though imagination is being slowed down by all the games and replaced more by mathematical and computerized games—which I love.

A man with an explosively sparkling sense of humor which brightens everything he thinks and does. He is so surreal, so far-out that sometimes neither he nor those around him know whether he is in control of his zaniness or his zaniness is in control of *him.* He is delightfully funny but he can also be exasperating: he is perfectly capable of serious thought and serious action, but the duration of his seriousness is unpredictable—at any moment he could be off on some private joke or could shift gears and start to put you on.

And yes, inside every clown there is a core of sadness, and he has his share of fear and sadness too. I suspect he has not yet learned to put these troublesome elements in the service of his art and creativity: he tends to look for a quick fix. In time, perhaps his comedy will acquire greater wisdom and greater complexity. Very much in his favor are his solid ties to family and friends from which he derives much security and joy.

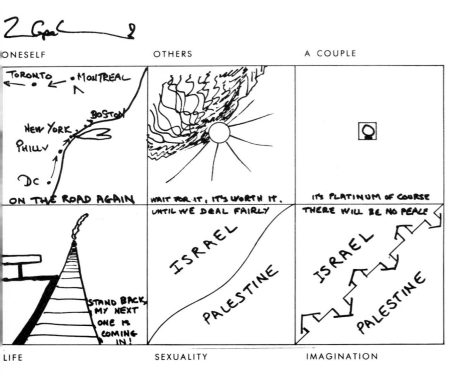

ONESELF   OTHERS   A COUPLE

TORONTO ← • MONTREAL
NEW YORK • BOSTON
PHILLY •
DC •
ON THE ROAD AGAIN

WAIT FOR IT, IT'S WORTH IT.
UNTIL WE DEAL FAIRLY

IT'S PLATINUM OF COURSE
THERE WILL BE NO PEACE

ISRAEL PALESTINE

ISRAEL PALESTINE

STAND BACK
MY NEXT
ONE IS
COMING
IN!

LIFE   SEXUALITY   IMAGINATION

1 I see myself as being to some extent working for others, making their careers happen. I'm myself always on the go. Sting is touring right now. So when I'm organizing a tour for an artist, I put myself in his shoes as if it was me.

2 I do so much business with my brother's family and friends that sometimes it is hard to distinguish who your true friends are. I always do try to distinguish them.

3 My relations with others are very important; at the end of the day relations are all what life's about.

4 My outlook of life: I've been through so many ups and downs in my life, I've seen so many trains leave! And I'm always looking forward to the next train coming in!

5 I would consider myself torn between chauvinistic relations of the past and understanding the new relation. I always consider my girlfriend as my girlfriend and want to help her all the way. And there is always a conflict between love and possession.

6 There will be no peace of mind, certainly looking at it politically. It will take a lot of imagination to work out the problem of the land, take the hatred and anger out. There is a solution to be found. In terms of my own imagination, I seem to like impossible challenges for things to make me take off. I'm at my best under attack.

▼ T H E   A N A L Y S I S

He describes himself as "to some extent working for others," but he is selling himself short. His drawings are those of a man with a clear, logical mind, with a fine grasp of complexities, with both analytic and combinatory skills—and he is a decisive man as well.

Perhaps because his work as facilitator and enabler of the work of others requires him to be behind the scenes, he underestimates his own contribution to the final product.

A forceful man but also a gentle man, and this combination is sometimes troublesome: he wants to be effective and to be effective he may have to throw his weight around a bit, yet he doesn't want to bruise egos— especially since he knows what a bruised ego feels like if, for instance, his work is taken for granted when it succeeds but he catches hell for the slightest glitch.

IAN COPELAND

MUSICAL ENTREPRENEUR/MANAGER

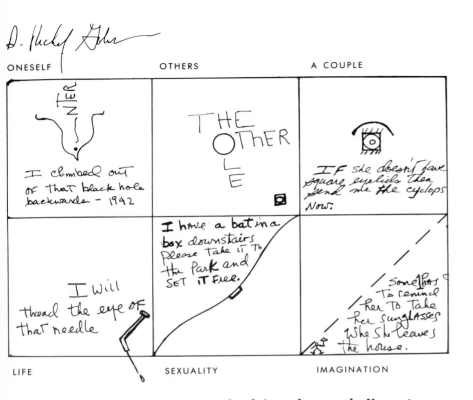

ONESELF | OTHERS | A COUPLE

I climbed out of that black hole backwards - 1942

THE OTHER HOLE

IF she doesn't have square eyelids then send me the cyclops Now.

I will thread the eye of that needle

I have a bat in a box downstairs Please take it to the Park and SET iT FREE.

Something To remind her To Take Her sunglasses When she leaves the house.

LIFE | SEXUALITY | IMAGINATION

1 I'm not trying to get back into the womb; I'm not in search of that and I'm glad to be out! The further I can get away from that darkness, the faster I can know what is going on in the world.

2 "The other hole." I see them at night. I see other people as miniature adventures, some of which turn out to be really boring or really exciting or really a waste of time, or what I wish was a wrong number. Or they all are an extension of Mr. K—the land surveyor.

3 I don't know anyone who has had an unsuccessful one or a successful one or one at all.

4 Flying around the planet all these years with this little metal bar trying to put it in its proper place—that's what a psychopath once said to me about creating a perfect work of art that he could leave behind.

5 Sexuality is a quality I constantly look for in others, just to make them feel self conscious! When I was younger I did it with mirrors, finding my own sexuality in someone else.

6 What's left of it.

It's all smashed up and dented, with millions of little pieces of it left on the highway. Spare parts—I will collect them someday and piece them all back together in my own image.

▼ T H E   A N A L Y S I S

This man has either elevated narcissism to an art form or he is a put-on artist laughing at the tester. The degree of self-centeredness in his comments is awesome: the universe starts and ends with him: people are little distractions to pick up, toy with, and dismiss; there is not much to expect, perhaps, in forming a couple; sex is simply a medium that lends itself very well to manipulation.

His association to "a perfect work of art" probably reflects his aspiration to perfection, to becoming the object of mass admiration and adulation.

The other side of this coin is, also in his own words, a self-experience of being "all smashed up and dented with millions of little pieces," which he will "collect some day and piece all back together" in his own image. It will take a lot of work!

And then again, perhaps he is pulling our leg.

ONESELF   OTHERS   A COUPLE

THE POINT IS THE POWER OF THE MIND. THE CENTER OF THE WORLD

THE EGG. THE POWER OF THE FEMALE

STRUCTURE: THE POWER OF CIVILIZATION

THE LINE: THE POWER OF SCIENCE

RANDOM: THE POWER OF NATURE

THE INFINITE: THE POWER OF GOD

LIFE   SEXUALITY   IMAGINATION

Well, it all obviously fell right into each square. *Perfect*. What more can I say?

Well, I must get back to my game of tennis. I was delighted, young girl.

This degree of self-satisfaction, particularly since it seems based on genuine accomplishment, can only be envied. He does not say much, but there is nothing retiring, nothing shy about this man's taciturnity. I think he feels that when one is in a state of harmony with mind, body, and environment, many words are superfluous.

Under the circumstances, I don't have much to say about him. At any rate, he seems too secure either to be offended by any critical comments or to be flattered by admiration.

78

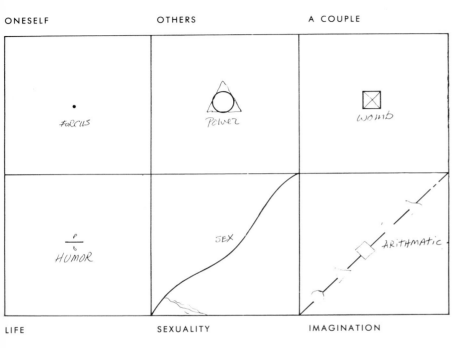

ONESELF   OTHERS   A COUPLE

FoRCUS   Power   womb

HUMOR   SEX   ARITHMATIC

LIFE   SEXUALITY   IMAGINATION

1 Not knowing the meaning, seeking, force is very important for me; it can be anything very analytical but at the same time intuitive. One is trying to focus on anything, focus for myself maybe? I don't know.

2 Power. I see this pyramid containing power and order.

3 Withdraw into myself. Symbiotic and afraid, not open, protected, insecure. I go into myself instead of letting myself out.

4 Humor. Very humorous, division, divided, divide everything equally.

5 I knew this one was sexuality. So once, someone collected drawings of cocks that each person had to draw. I only drew a part of it.

6 I saw the drawing, everything broken inside . . . , I linked them all together with powerful symbols—circle, triangle, square. Symbols are so powerful.

▼ THE ANALYSIS

A good example of a test performance that stymies a psychologist. His drawings are minimalist, his comments are distilled abstractions. Does he really think about himself and about life in the condensed form we see in his test record? Or is all this a smoke screen behind which he is hiding? If the abstractions are, in fact, summary statements rather than camouflage, do they express well-thought-out ideas and concepts or are they buzz words that conceal the lack of real thought? In the absence of a face-to-face talk or at least of some opportunity to question him further, it is impossible to say.

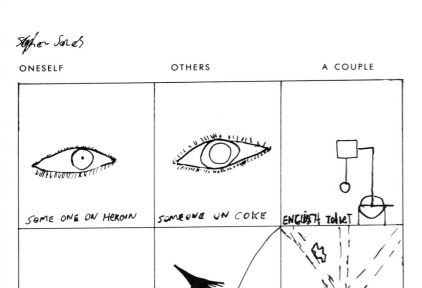

ONESELF — SOME ONE ON HEROIN

OTHERS — SOMEONE ON COKE

A COUPLE — ENGLISH TOILET

LIFE — AT A PARTY

SEXUALITY — THE SIDE OF A BIG BROKEN HEART

IMAGINATION — ENGLISH FLAG

1 I used to be like that a long time.

2 Others? They're all right. I don't mind them. But I don't like French people. I like American people.

3 I don't think couples are happy. They are for a little while, then it kind of gets boring and they start looking around again. Big eyes!

4 I guess it's—I'm not going to say that life is a great party. Does that look like a champagne glass? I was getting lost there for a second. Life is meant to have fun.

5 It seems like sexual attitude. I love sex. As much as you can!

6 Not much, it looks like me. I've run out of ideas by the time it's got to here. That's why they put it last. I don't know, it's better to have imagination than someone who just copies—I don't like who just copies—tricky for imagination.

▼ THE ANALYSIS

Of his six drawings, three refer to mind-altering substances and his comments reflect a way of looking at things in terms of their being "boring" or "fun." It all adds up to strong emphasis on direct and intense sensory experience and lack of interest in complex thought, in introspective reflection, in verbal process.

Therefore I think that his creative outlet has intensity and spontaneity, but that when he is not busy with his art, he may experience boredom, restlessness, perhaps depression. He probably makes a great companion, but his friendships may lack depth.

His view of "couples" is interesting: he says they are "happy for a little while, then it kind of gets boring and they start looking around again." Is he an embittered cynic, or is he a clear-visioned realist? Let the reader decide *this* one.

STEVE JONES

MUSICIAN, THE SEX PISTOLS

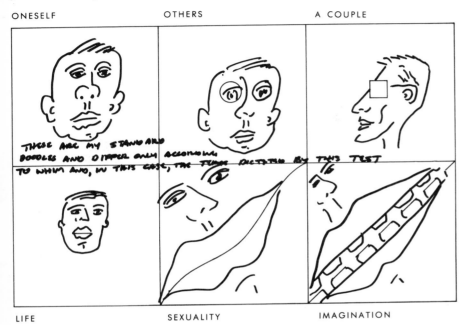

Fran Lebowitz (signature)

ONESELF   **OTHERS**   **A COUPLE**

THESE ARE MY STANDARD DOODLES AND I OFFER ONLY ACCOMPANIMENT TO WHOM AND, IN THIS CASE, THE THINGS DICTATED BY THIS TEST

LIFE   **SEXUALITY**   **IMAGINATION**

1 I think it's more indicative of my philosophy of doodling than my philosophy of life. This juncture is a philosophy of doodling. I always draw these things. I draw hundreds of them a day. Do you care to buy any of them? I don't actually think I see myself like this. I don't think I'm this merry at the moment.

2 Those are just round eyes. Just a circle, just the vagaries of ink. I think this is perhaps less telling than one might hope.

3 This is how I see marriage. This, I think—marriages with only one person in them. Yes, yes, this is the perfect marriage. I see others, this one's interesting.

4 This is the smallest. Well, it's the cheeriest. I'm surprised to see that . . . figure out what this one is.

5 Sexuality. A mouth is appropriate. A happy one.

6 In imagination, the teeth. I didn't quite know what to do with that jagged line. I think that in most cases it's better to curb it —I wouldn't necessarily say I do. I think people are altogether too fantasy-ridden as it is. I think it's always the same ones, actually.

Yes, those are the limits of imagination. Yes, that's because people are more limited than one might hope. There are very few people in whose imagination one is interested. So in general, I think imagination in others should be discouraged. And I can see that you're probably more charitable than I am. But also you're much younger. You may come to this. Well, I think it's inevitable that—I'm thirty-seven—that you'll come to this conclusion.

Do you then show this to some sort of psychiatrist or something?

▼ T H E   A N A L Y S I S

An intelligent woman who uses her intelligence in the service of coping with her anger. Her principal tool is her humor,

84

and she has a knack of transforming cynicism and sarcasm into more acceptable but still quite abrasive irony.

Some of her anger is self-directed, and there may well be times when her defenses fail and the ironic stance no longer works—at those times she becomes quite depressed. Still, there is probably enough resilience that sooner or later she becomes again a provocative and funny woman.

Look at her drawing on the fifth square, at the huge, soft, sensuous mouth which, she says, is "appropriate" to sexuality. Well, yes. But then look at the next square: there are huge, sharp teeth behind those lips. The mouth that kisses can also bite. And our subject can be very biting indeed.

Self-centered. About other people she says that they are "more limited than one might hope," and that there are "very few . . . in whose imagination one is interested." Some of this contemptuous, arrogant stance is

defensive in that it protects her from disappointment. If you can't expect much from others, how can they let you down and hurt you by their neglect or rejection?

FRAN LEBOWITZ

WRITER

Nile Rodgers

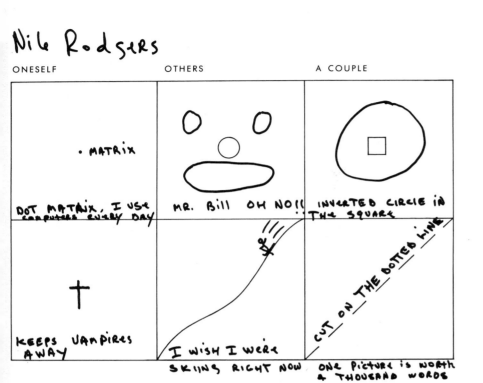

ONESELF

· MATRIX

DOT MATRIX, I use computers every day

†

KEEPS VAMPIRES AWAY

LIFE

OTHERS

MR. BILL OH NO!!

I WISH I WERE SKIING RIGHT NOW

SEXUALITY

A COUPLE

INVERTED CIRCLE IN THE SQUARE

CUT ON THE DOTTED LINE

ONE PICTURE IS WORTH A THOUSAND WORDS

IMAGINATION

1 I certainly can't say that this is the definite vision of myself, but I see how it fits into it. I consider myself high-tech and low-tech. I use technology for my feelings.

2 Strange, I'm not critical of others. I'm very forgiving and liberal. I would never criticize someone openly, inside maybe, but in silence.

3 Relations are not necessarily a perfect fit.

4 Ah, ah, ah. Guess that I am a literal kind of guy. I saw a line! Can't intellectualize. I can maybe say that I had a Roman Catholic education. Fear of God. It's a visual thing. Yeah, I'm afraid of vampires.

5 Sexuality: Full speed ahead!

6 Interesting, it was totally visual when I saw it. Then I remembered this anecdote told to me years ago. Melvin Van Peebles, a young black director who had a tattoo done around his neck like a perforated chain. And as part of the chain, he had written: "cut along the dotted line." When he left for Paris, maybe was it for the guillotine? I loved that story.

86

This man is trying to tame a turbulent emotional life by means of intellectual mastery. I think he is trying to reason with a volcano of feelings, with the results you would expect.

His likes, his dislikes, his passions, his aversions are all powerful as are his fears. A successful man, often on an emotional high but with a dread of falling, with a suspicion that he is a square peg in a round hole, and a worry that the greater the crowned head the likelier it is to be sent to the guillotine.

We each have our tricks to keep our private vampires away, and this man's methods seem to work as well as anybody's.

NILE RODGERS

MUSIC PRODUCER

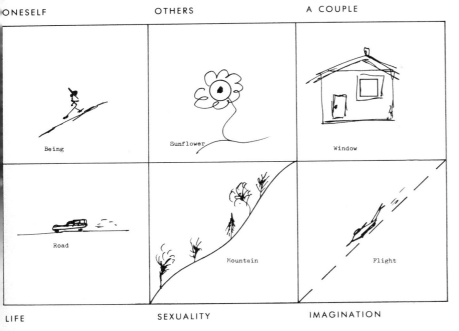

ONESELF   OTHERS   A COUPLE

Being

Sunflower

Window

LIFE   SEXUALITY   IMAGINATION

Road

Mountain

Flight

1 A being walking; the dot would be a human head, basically a being.

2 That's how I see a sunflower.

3 A window, preferably in a house.

4 Car indicates a road; anything flat or straight would be a road. It's not in the linear sense, it's in the lateral sense; it cannot be represented graphically.

5 This will always be a mountain to me, either in summer or winter, and it's the mountain I've seen.

6 The notion of "steep" is always connected with the sense of flight. I don't see as graphically as represented.

▼ THE ANALYSIS

A man who hid behind a mask! Yes, we all present masks to the world and suit our actions to the circumstances, but in his case the mask was not an adaptation; it was a deception. Yet, the deceptive mask also gives teasing hints of what it may have been hiding.

He was a man who sent out self-contradicting signals probably because his experience of himself was full of painful contradictions. Or could he have been perpetrating a colossal joke on all of us?

More a spectator of life than an actor—but an intensely involved spectator. He was energetic, but some of the energy was diverted into fighting its own source, just as he was ambitious with a strong self-defeating streak: a mixture of tenderness and hardness.

The test record makes me extremely curious about the subject. I would like to have known him. I suspect, though, that more time spent with him would have left me more rather than less puzzled about him.

JERZY KOSINSKI

WRITER

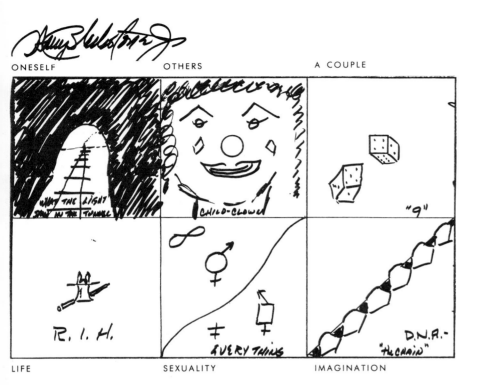

LIFE   SEXUALITY   IMAGINATION

1 Now the first one, the point. I thought of that as being the point of a train in the distance and I envisioned what it must be like. We all the time think of the light at the end of the tunnel, and when I thought of what it must be like if I were the light in the tunnel, see what was coming toward me—as we're always trying to see the light at the end of the tunnel.

2 The second one with the child is the way I see others. People are fun, they're fun to be with, they're joyous, they're smiling. I enjoy, you know, personal relationships with people, and although I don't like to think of people as being hard, this struck me as a hard-nose—that circle—and I built around that with what was the eyes and the features of the typical Grimaldi kind of profile. I never think of clowns as being sad. Clowns to me are always happy. They represent happiness, they represent the circus, they represent joy, the childlike enjoyment we all have, fantasy. I don't count it all as being sad. I think if

people inside of the clown are being sad, it's because their way to express their sadness is to pretend to be happy. Yeah, but then I never think of the clown itself, that character, as being sad.

3 I saw the square as part of a pair of dice, and I happened to have chosen the four dots on the original square and the five dots on the other die, so that together they make a nine, which is approaching perfection, although I didn't realize what the implications of this would be because you didn't explain that, but that nine out of ten, I figure, is for that. Well, this is my third marriage that I'm currently involved with. My third and final marriage I might add, because if I don't get it right this time, I'm not going to try it again. We've been happily married for nearly sixteen years; we have four wonderful children, and four out of five isn't bad. And our relationship is under great pressure all of the time, because we both live together, work together, create together. My wife is my number-one assistant in my show. She's the one that gets sawed in half at every performance. And recently when I was asked what the secret of our success has been, I said it's the fact that in all of our years of being together, we've never had a serious conversation. So, that's it. She's the five and I'm the four.

4 I saw the top of that horizontal line as being the brim of a hat and I started to make the hat the other direction, when I realized that the hat actually inverted itself as I was watching. And out of any empty hat, of course, a magician holding a rabbit, and a little wand, or cane, or authority. My rabbit's just coming out of the hat. That's how I see life. Certain things pop out of it. That there's always something else in the bottom of that hat that will appear. It's the cornucopia, it's the Pandora's box. But it's also that the hat is the thing from which we produce all of the things that make my professional and personal life, which are very much one and the same. I literally live and work magically my life as a performer. I mean, I'm not one to fool myself into believing that the magic I do on stage is anything other than an entertainment form. I do nothing that is supernatural. I only do those things which are enjoyable and which hope-

HARRY BLACKSTONE, JR.

MAGICIAN

fully bring pleasure and enjoyment to audiences.

5 Yes, because this is everything: the male, the female, birth, death, infinity. All of these things are part of life, whether it's from one side or the other. Both of these symbols—this being the symbol for female, that being the symbol for male—the same kind of thing in reverse in which, whatever your position might be in the world, whether you're a square peg in a round hole or a round peg in a square hole—pardon the sexual allusion in that—it's everything. It's infinity, it's birth and death and life and all of those things which, in spite of what seems to be a separation that's imaginary, you could move across, back and forth, across that line as you will. And the last on this continuity line.

6 DNA is deoxyribonucleic acid. It's the basic material from which all of the genes and chromosomes, all of the human characteristics come. The DNA chain is what makes up all the human traits in genetics. That chain, that continuity, determines what everything is from our eye color to our grandchildren. That is the true source of imagination, because this is the basic nuclear building

block from which all living things have come. Although recently, scientifically, they believe that certain forms of clay have the ability to capture certain forms of moisture and, thus, will create the chemicals that give essence to life. Now, this is the scientific rather than the theological approach. In fact, just in today's May 5 edition of *The New York Times,* there's an article about this particular material. But anyway, this is the chain, and in this chain are the chromosomes and the genes that go together and that make up human life.

▼ T H E   A N A L Y S I S

A great deal of talk, but much of it serves to conceal rather than reveal. As if by repeating something a sufficient number of times and with sufficient emphasis, you can make it come true.

He protests too much when he insists that "clowns are always happy." In fact, neither clowns nor he are *always* happy but, as he says, "their way to express their sadness is to pretend to be happy."

I don't mean to imply that this is a fundamentally sad person—I don't think he suffers more than most of us. However, he is adamant in his desire not to show any weakness, any sadness, any worry, any dissatisfaction. He insists on seeing life as always providing some pleasant surprise coming out of the hat just when you think there is nothing there anymore.

Is it excessive fear of death? Is he denying the limits and limitation of life, its finiteness, the unknown? There is a quest for some framework, some system—scientific and/or religious—which will add meaning to his existence and reduce his existential anxiety.

His marital life and his professional life appear to be in good order. I hope he finds greater spiritual satisfaction as well.

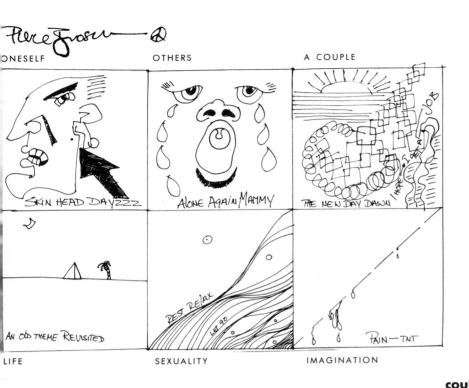

ONESELF　　　　　OTHERS　　　　　A COUPLE

SKIN HEAD DAYZZZ

Alone Again MAMMY

THE NEW DAY DAWN

AN OLD THEME REVISITED

REST RELAX
LET GO

PAIN—TNT

LIFE　　　　　SEXUALITY　　　　　IMAGINATION

1 I was a skinhead at one time. I draw, and I've been drawing earrings on people for ages. Today I put this earring in because I'm going to an audition today, and I thought, hey, it'll look good. What a coincidence!

2 "Alone again," I mean, really I was awfully sad, and I don't really relate to that one.

How others are to me. I don't think they cry. I cry. Yeah, when I look at this, I look at my life. Yes, I'm more melancholic than my wife. She's up and open, and I'm the kind of dark, brooding Irish.

3 I'm very regimented. I want everything done precisely, and I like order, and I like repetition, I guess. Whereas Cassy is much more sensuous, and I suppose that's where these squiggly lines come from: the blending in of the two. Somehow, there's a harmony between us, because we're a good combination together, and so far the sun has never set in our relationship.

And "the new day dawn, I hope I get a job." Well, there are four or five jobs—four jobs—especially at the moment which are very important jobs. Yes, I'm the squares and she's these kind of squiggly things that go around my life and keeps all my squares in order, I guess.

4 Life. "An old theme revisited." I keep on going back on it and—wow!—there's nothing in it. There's a loneliness to the picture, alone. I was brought up very much alone. I was an only child. And the moon, the half-moon, I don't know what that could represent—my father. And the solitary palm tree could be representing my mother.

"An old theme." That's amazing for life—just that one sentence and I've got the meaning of the square. I keep on going back on it and I dwell on it. I suppose that's my childhood.

5 "Rest, relax, let go . . ." sexuality. Well, we have a good sexual life together, I don't know what to say, I mean—you want more? Well, I hope there's a certain sensuality in what I've done. There's certainly an accent. I find it very difficult talking when it comes to sexuality. It's such a private thing and it's such a thing that you don't dwell on. Yeah, I'm

a rowdy bugger at times!
6 "Pain—TNT." Again talking about it. What to say? Some people can spend their entire lives avoiding it; some can't live with it; some don't even use it. I use it all the time. I feel I don't use it enough at times, so I go wild with it in the paintings that I do, or in the poetry that I write. In the work that I do as an actor I feel maybe it's been stifled an awful lot in the last few years, only because I've been in a regimented t.v. series, locked into it. I've been kind of nullified. But, I'm out of it now. My life has blossomed in the past year.

▼ THE ANALYSIS

A multitalented man who has a lot going for him—a good marriage, professional success, appreciation of art, youth, presumably good health. . . .

Why then the streak of melancholy that is there like the constant drone of a bagpipe? Obviously, he is an actor, and like all actors, except for a few superstars, he has to audition, to be rejected, occasionally has to work in stuff he isn't proud of, to remain idle between jobs sometimes—but all that comes with the territory.

Through his drawings and his comments he reveals the still very strong hold of a troubled past: unhappy childhood? anti-social adolescence? Probably nothing strikingly out of the ordinary, but he is still haunted by too many ghosts. Fortunately, most people ultimately do find the exorcism that works best for them.

Bret Easton Ellis

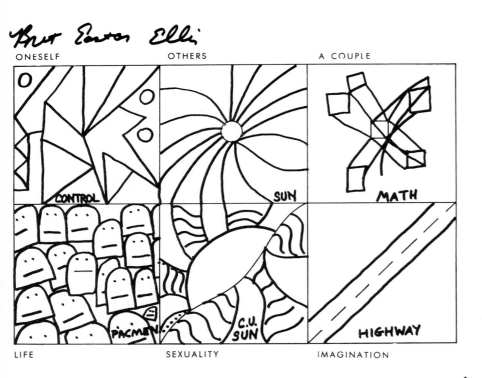

ONESELF	OTHERS	A COUPLE
CONTROL	SUN	MATH
PACMEN	C.U. SUN	HIGHWAY
LIFE	SEXUALITY	IMAGINATION

1 I can't see what the drawing started off with. This is very strange, because for a long time I thought that I wasn't in control of my life—in business, my agent and editor and publisher and lawyers and accountants and parents had control over it. This drawing says—what? That I'm controlled by others and that I'm trying to take over?

2 This one also confused me. I guess I depend very much on my friends. I need them. The sun sustains life and without friends I wouldn't be around? Others bring out qualities in me, friends bring out my personality? Yet this is strange because I'm also very good at being alone.

3 This drawing is a mess. I didn't know how to go about it and I couldn't finish it. I wanted to draw a perfect shape and gave up after trying several times. I suppose it has something to do with always being very bad at math as a child and—I guess I still am. I'm also—pessimistic? I'm not a firm believer? I look at my generation, tend to think that the couples I see around me are seldom really in love. Often unhealthy reasons keep them together. My parents were separated when I was a child. Watching their relationship not work may have helped form this attitude?

4 I was thinking of two other ways to name this picture, either *Toast* or *Thumbs*. I ended up calling it *Pacmen*. Why? Well, they all look alike, but the one in the middle is the first I drew; he looks the happiest. The baby I did last. So, I feel, what? My life is unchanging? I'm verbally self-expressive, yet why do they all have closed mouths? I can't imagine them talking. No secrets, no mystery. I don't believe in God. Life is a series of random events. Life is not permanent. Why did I agree to do this?!

5 No comment, really. I didn't know what to name it. The "C.U." stands for *close-up*. And it's funny I joined it together with the second panel. The sun is joining the other drawing. Sexuality and friendship should go hand in hand? You want to have sex more with someone who is also a friend rather than with a total stranger?

6 I find it important. It's needed, yet it's also a

curse of sorts. Imagination brings you to great places, magical grounds and it's positive? But people who don't have imagination don't travel and must have terribly boring dreams? When you are imagining you tend to dwell upon things which are a waste of time to contemplate? Imagination is vital for me? Then, why do I phrase that last sentence as a question?

▼ T H E   A N A L Y S I S

It is almost as if our test has caught this young man in the very process of growing up, of his moving toward greater maturity in every way.

He is perceptive and imaginative, and has extraordinary verbal facility with which to express his perception and his imagination. His need for others is in fine equilibrium with his ability to be alone. He derives nurturance from friends and nurtures them in return. He is progressively taking more control of his life, but with no evidence of being a "control freak." His talent and his high level of energy make for a very felicitous combination, and he is generous with his talent.

He is also young. He has not reached any stability in his view of what couples should be all about, of sexuality, of family—but then, he is only in his twenties. Plenty of reason to be optimistic about his future.

ONESELF | OTHERS | A COUPLE

SMITH-CORONA

GREAT HORNED OWL

"With an olive, please."

THE PALACE OF WISDOM →

THE ROAD OF EXCESS ---

THE PATH OF RIGHTEOUSNESS

LIFE | SEXUALITY | IMAGINATION

1 If this is myself, it firstly indicates that I'm not eternal, and unfortunately that I'm not as wise as the great owl. I definitely think that the owl goes in a roundabout circle within the square of life, flying between wisdom and excess.

2 I usually see others over a drink—at dinner somewhere. If not, I'm at home working all day in solitude and quiet.

3 If you are a writer, your typewriter eventually comes between you and all your loved ones. Relations are a pool of betrayal or trust and relations are wonderful and exquisite tortures. My major competition is writing.

4 "The palace of wisdom" is a quote from William Blake. That's probably what I was thinking of, but I'm sure that there's a much more direct route to both extremes.

5 Nice curve! Well, I must be heterosexual.

6 Imagination. Well, I guess it's the most direct route to any place, something which isn't surprising for a writer.

▼ THE ANALYSIS

Creativity and execution are nicely balanced here. This man is inventive and open to inspiration: he comes up with original, imaginative ideas. At the same time, he has respect for and mastery of technique: he knows how to give his creativity the shape necessary to make it accessible to a wide audience.

A man whose Apollonian and Dionysian components are in harmony, probably in every aspect of his life. In addition to his work, his friendships and more intimate relations probably also reflect this fortunate balance between feeling and thought, between emotion and reason.

Of course, there are those who will be critical of him: he is probably too cerebral for the histrionically inclined and too starry-eyed for the grammarians of life.

JAY MCINERNEY

ONESELF　　　　　　OTHERS　　　　　A COUPLE

it's all a stunt

threatening fish

home life is magic

delivering flowers in your dream

inter-city existence

LIFE　　*splat after bite*　　SEXUALITY　　　　IMAGINATION

three stars at an early age

1 How long can I continue to get away with all this?

2 I always think everyone is trying to rip me off.

3 If only I can keep the wife quiet and asleep perhaps I can finish my painting.

4 The story of my life, forever on the move.

5 Flower power!

6 Your guess is as good as mine.

▼ T H E   A N A L Y S I S

Life is a juggling act and he has a lot of balls in the air. His performance is evidently very successful—how could it fail with the energy, vitality, creativity, and talent he exudes? Yet, he is worried that his success may be a stunt he is getting away with, that the whole act will blow up in his face, that the sharks who are after him will rip him up and destroy him.

Sometimes he feels in danger of being overwhelmed by his own energy, by his perpetual motion, by his flood of imagery.

However, he knows how to channel this power productively, and he is protected by a lovely ability to be involved and yet take some distance and by a delightful sense of humor which permits him to not take himself too seriously while working very seriously indeed.

Is it necessary to note that his expressive talent is graphic rather than verbal?

D A M I A N   E L W E S

P A I N T E R

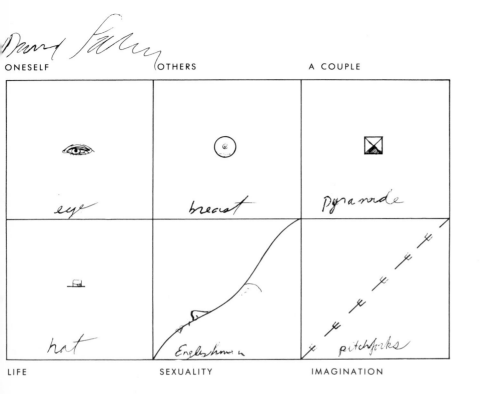

ONESELF | OTHERS | A COUPLE

eye | breast | Pyramide

hat | Englishman | pitchforks

LIFE | SEXUALITY | IMAGINATION

1 Eye.

2 Breast.

3 Pyramid.

4 Hat.

5 Englishman.

6 Pitchforks.

▼ T H E   A N A L Y S I S

An intelligence with a strong component of whimsy. He has the ability to suggest and imply a great deal more than he states explicitly. Just as in dreams a simple everyday object or image can carry a heavy load of evocation, of implication, of mystery and revelation at the same time, his productions, even when minimal, have the richness of surrealistic and conceptual art.

Minds like these are not open to being second-guessed. They contain more variety and complexity than the outsider can hope to penetrate. Asking him for greater clarity would, in all likelihood, simply provoke him to become more elusive and cryptic.

Karole Armitage (signature)

ONESELF	OTHERS	A COUPLE

A Noh mask of the character who had a small piece of cloth which when it was wound around her back way to small to meet in front of her breasts. This represents the love of her life which was never requited.

A lonely octopus on the bottom of the sea

Abstraction

Beginning of a cartoon drawing.

Beach with a sculpture made of driftwood and two stones.

Highway across the desert.

LIFE	SEXUALITY	IMAGINATION

Noh is a kind of form of dance drama six hundred years old and many of the characters wear a mask and there are stories about people's lives that have come back from the dead, reminiscing about what happened to them in their lives. So, this one is just a female character. Oh, it's very easy to conjure up relationships with anything. I mean, I think that's what you're always trying to do in making art. But, so why not fantasize here and use the imagination? Well, Noh, this idea of Noh mask. It's interesting that that coincidence happened in this square, because you're thinking so much, when you look at something on stage, you can only tell the story in really one or two characters at the most. And this Noh drama being about—through ritualized gesture—being about suppressed emotion, it becomes intensely dramatic to the spectator, and it's always talking about incidents of real life experience, through a great deal of imagination.

And I feel so lucky that I did this in this place, because what I'm always trying to do in dance is to use images that do have that kind of suppressed but very violently emotional impact. Especially modern dance. Yes, without it being acting, through. Never, you should never be acting. You should really come through half abstraction, half symbol, half realism; but through movement and rhythm—that is what conveys the human content, and that's exactly what Noh, I think, does and achieves better than any other form of performance in the world.

The very first time I saw this—it must have been in '84, and I've been interested in that form ever since. It's Japanese and it's, as I said, six hundred years old and the people who do it now are from the same families that did it six hundred years ago. It's been handed down. They wear the same clothes; the masks they wear were made then also.

It's a very traditional thing, as I say, it's the greatest example of what imagination can be on stage, because they start talking and time is telescoped. Suddenly, you're ten years in the past, then you jump twelve years in the future, then you jump ten minutes before, and this is all happening through this incredibly codified language of gesture and voice, and the speaking imagination is incredible, the music is very, very beautiful.

And it's always the story of a person who's traveling—and you see the person travel onto the stage, and they ask a local person, "What is this mound of Earth I see here, what is it about this place?" And they will say, "This is the grave of so-and-so, and you see this vine growing. That vine grew as soon as this person died." And then, the local person telling this traveler about the place leaves for a minute, comes back with a mask on and an incredible elaborate robe—and in fact that is the person that is in that grave—comes back and dances and acts out the story of a love that was so demanding that this vine grew and now, even in their death, they're being constantly strangled by this love that is too intense and that they can't get free of.

So, they're always tales of after death, of these people about their lives. They're so poignant; they're riveting—and it's in very, very slow motion, which is also very strange. It's incredibly—. It's the most spare, the most beautiful condensed kind of stage experience. So, I suppose this what I love most in the world right now. So, it's very interesting that I put that for myself. I mean, it would be my greatest dream to be able to do something, even with a little bit of that contemplative—. It's like an opiate, you get addicted. Time is so different watching it—I'd like to be able to addict people that way. They always move very slowly. It's amazing the way they move their hands. They are very concentrated. Lonely. Well, yes, we're alone, all trying to figure out what life is about and then, every time we get one glimpse, it changes, and then we have to try another tactic. I think I can do either, to tell the truth. And I need a great deal of time that is very, very quiet for the imagination to be freed. It's hard for it to be freed in a room full of people.

And yet, what really interests me in dance and—I'm talking about myself—is the very intense relationship you have with other people, what they look like, how their body looks, what their personality is like and how it makes them move in a certain way. And it's an incredibly intimate kind of unrequited love in a way, because you really do love those people and what they are as their entire being and how that then turns into something kind of ritualized that becomes the dance, but that is very much drawn from themselves.

So, you need—I think you have to care very much for people, probably, to be a choreographer, even though I am a very solitary person also. I think it's the most revealing possible exposure that any human being lets themselves up—be seen, you know, be seen under . . . It's like a microscope revealing their most private psychological selves. You see everything in how a person moves. It's never abstract. Dance is never totally abstract because the inflection that a person gives in moving, the way they hold themselves, say so much about them, and that's what I adore. Dancers are very aware of that, though no one ever talks about it.

It sometimes produces a great deal of neurosis or confusion, because they're always trying to be perfect in a technical way. Technique is the abstract side, because that's just the mechanics of making you move, but you feel so much failure when you can't move exactly the way this outside idea is, and yet it's by using that outside idea that you can reveal the most about yourself. So, there's this kind of constant back and forth, often a real confusing thing. It's very, very, very frustrating, awful, yeah.

I think this kind of dancing has a short life span. I mean, I'm doing very violent movement. Probably the most violent. It's extreme. The legs go very, very high, and the speed is very intense, and the positions are often really kind of wrenching to the body, because you move from one kind of extreme position to another very quickly, and throwing in often very kind of funky syncopated rhythms. I mean, you could do something else, something again, going back to something like Noh. They believe you can dance at least into your forties and still be very good . . . very slow movements, no demands on the hips, no jumping, none of that kind of stuff. And so much of a performance really is

about beauty, and when you're forty-five, your face just doesn't look as good, let alone the rest of you. Yes, and there are examples of people whose aesthetic can take on a lot—it can take on age or it can take on some kind of dramatic side to it that makes it work, but I don't think mine is that way. At least at this point it certainly isn't. Like Martha Graham, but she is a different generation and, I mean, they believed that artists had a kind of calling. It was almost like a religious fervor, and they had to make people into converts, and it was like a temple; it was a religion, definitely.

And in our day and age, I think we feel that artists have different temperaments, in the 80s. That's a very old fashioned idea about what an artist is, and I don't think we can feel like we're on this kind of great cause that people have to adhere to. That feels too egomaniacal somehow.

▼ THE ANALYSIS

A woman of enormous self-discipline. She mobilizes a great deal of energy and channels it into almost minimalist output. Her voluble comment may appear to be contradicting my label "minimalist," but her primary outlet is not verbal: she distills ideas into gestures or into concepts that find graphic or spatial expression.

There is a very complex and very creative intelligence and a very multi-dimensional and very powerful emotional drive behind her art, which succeeds in transmuting much inner conflict and inner pain into beauty. Note how she draws "a lonely octopus at the bottom of the sea," "a sculpture made of driftwood" on an unpopulated beach, and "a desert"—all desolate images—and how there are no human figures at all except for a stylized mask and "the beginning of a cartoon drawing." But there is a highway across the desert, the lonely octopus is full of lively motion, and the driftwood and stones have been turned into art.

She suffers, she hurts, she has a turbulent inner life, and at the same time she cares, she loves, she feels compassion, she works hard, and out of it all, she creates beauty.

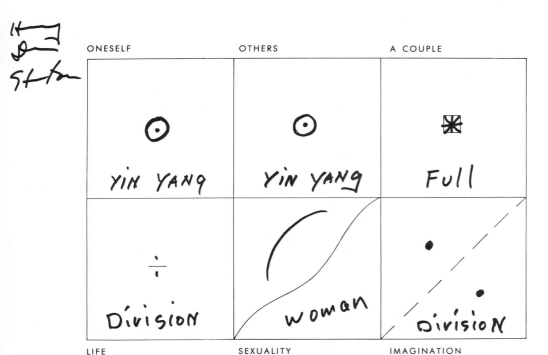

ONESELF	OTHERS	A COUPLE
⊙	⊙	✳
YIN YANG	YIN YANG	Full
÷		• •
Division	woman	Division
LIFE	SEXUALITY	IMAGINATION

1 We all are yin and yang.

2 Others? That's pretty goddamn basic.

3 Couple is "full?" I guess so!

4 "Division?" I guess that goes with my career. Seems healthy, I don't know. Division means the process of dividing, the state of being divided, the act, process of —the instance of dividing.

5 Speaks for itself, this one.

6 Imagination. Division again. Diversity, I guess.

A test record like this one frustrates by its brevity, especially in the absence of any other information about the subject: if only I could ask him a couple of questions!

The only concern I find expressed in the test is the quest for union, for completion, for a harmonious fusion of opposites. Is the persistence of this theme throughout the test (not only "Yin and Yang" and "division" but even a simplified *Union* Jack) because this man is totally obsessed with it? Or (and I think more likely) is it that after agreeing to comply with test instructions, he quickly became bored with the whole thing!

HARRY DEAN STANTON

ACTOR

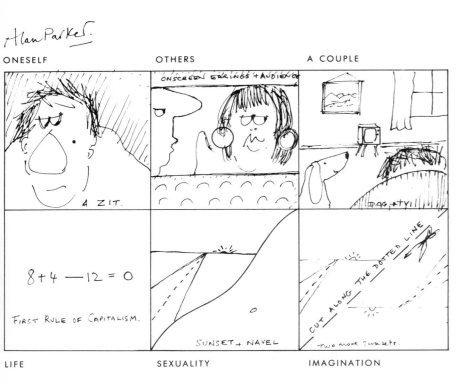

ONESELF   OTHERS   A COUPLE

A ZIT.

ONSCREEN EARRINGS + AUDIENCE

DIGG + TV!

8 + 4 — 12 = 0

FIRST RULE OF CAPITALISM.

SUNSET + NAVEL

CUT ALONG THE DOTTED LINE

Two more Sunsets.

LIFE   SEXUALITY   IMAGINATION

Alan Parker.

1 Yes. The first one is how I see myself. Oh, I suppose so, yeah. Insecure.

2 Others! Well, then it is pretty weird, isn't it? I see others as images as opposed to reality, I suppose. I don't know.

3 This is home? Yes, couples. Whoa . . . I drew my dog instead of my wife. I suppose it's pretty significant. This is weird, this is strange actually.

4. Life. That's me struggling with working in America, I suppose, in a way. This probably preoccupies me right now. It's just that you are struggling away here, because of money, money to earn, money to make your movies. But what does it add up to? Does it add up to you doing better work? Maybe that's something I have got to struggle with every day. I don't know.

5 Sexuality. "Sunset plus navel." That's okay. I mean, sunset, that's quite nice.

6 "Cut along the dotted line." Schizophrenia! The images are the same, except one is upside down. Sunset, I enjoy the sunset, actually.

This man's creativity and competence are in strong contrast to his sense of insecurity.

He derives satisfaction from his craft, not only because he is competent, but also because in his professional activity he can deal with people from a safe psychological distance even when physically close.

His marriage probably represents a satisfying but delicate balance in which the strengths and weaknesses both of the husband and of the wife fit nicely but precariously together.

There is something of a boy in this grown-up man—both in the sense of vulnerability and in the sense of playfulness, imaginativeness, adventurousness.

A L A N P A R K E R

DIRECTOR

[signature]

ONESELF | OTHERS | A COUPLE

?		
Point d'interrogation	HELLO	2001
DAMIENS HOUSE	SLEEPING	BRUM BRUM

LIFE | SEXUALITY | IMAGINATION

1 Interrogation mark, enigma for you and me.

2 Shalom. I think she wants to dance. Shall I ask her?

3 "2001." Well, what do relationships have in common with monkeys and monoliths? My comment: they have a lot in common with m and m!

4 In reflection: Damien's house is a once and future forum; Damien was once a future honorary counsel. Happy days will be here again, we don't know when, we don't know where.

5 It really says "let's fuck" but I did not write it so as not to embarrass my hostess. She's not really sleeping, she's getting it up the bum.

6 Imagination is the grand prix, "le coup du champion"—that's what they call the European cup.

A talented, creative man who views the world through lenses of cynicism, a man who defies conventional and traditional forms, but in the process makes an icon of his iconoclasm. In his work he is likely to experiment with new twists before he is settled in any one form. In his personal relationships, I suspect that he keeps people guessing about where they stand with him. A man still in the process of maturing.

JULIAN SANDS

ACTOR

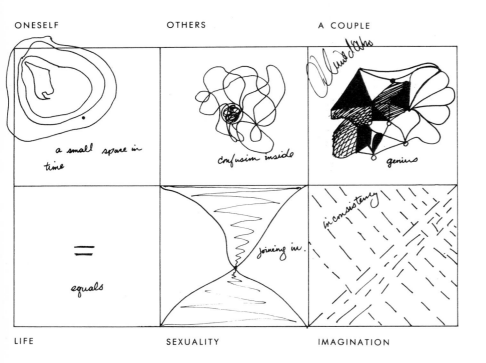

ONESELF

a small space in time

OTHERS

confusion inside

A COUPLE

genius

LIFE

equals

=

SEXUALITY

joining in.

IMAGINATION

inconsistency

1 I see myself contributing in space and time. I live each day as it comes my way, in spontaneous authenticity. I want to be a giver and not a taker, because there are too many takers in the world that suck the planet with their greed—sucking the planet for their need of power and their obsessions.

2 They look at you in the eye. Confusion is being cut off from the ability to live naturally, because it blocks life with analytical behavior. It's a misconception of one's being. It's also not understanding where one's at or from. Moment to moment, it's not being at one with your partner. If you don't express it, you get tangled in it.

3 Relationships are something that one needs desperately to bring out the different qualities in each one of us. That's why all relationships are different. Some relations are predictable because you're looking for something you can't find in yourself and that you'll never find in the other, if it's not in you.

4 Life equals what you put into it. If you set high goals for your abilities and work towards them, you'll get to where your dream takes you, otherwise you'll live your life in a closet and wake up one day and realize that your actions speak louder than words.

5 Sexuality is a need in all of us to let ourselves go. Your real sexuality will come out in your fantasies, because one doesn't always have the guts to express themselves. That's why fantasies are make believe. Celibacy is for the brave.

6 Imagination is being able to visualize what is not in front of you and create a reality within that empty space.

A young woman struggling to acquire a strong sense of identity and of her place in the world, and succeeding in this struggle.

She has considerable analytical ability but for some reason finds her own analytical skills suspect—she wants to rely on intuition at the expense of thought.

A hard worker; she takes her career seriously and works at it conscientiously, without expecting success on a silver platter.

She is not *completely* comfortable with her sexuality (on the other hand, who *is?*), and there is a quality of unsettledness, of flux, in her sexual experience. Perhaps she was tested during an interesting phase in her life.

All in all, a nicely balanced individual who should be encouraged to develop her intellect as well as her intuition—right now, she is blocking out one very important asset.

OLIVIA D'ABO

ACTRESS

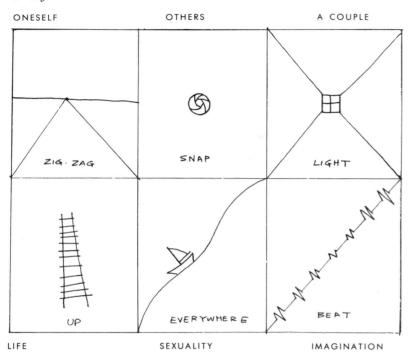

ONESELF	OTHERS	A COUPLE
ZIG-ZAG	SNAP	LIGHT
UP	EVERYWHERE	BEAT
LIFE	SEXUALITY	IMAGINATION

1 **"Zig zag."** **Zig-zagging through life, I guess. At the point of no return.**

2 **"Snap." I see others through a lens; it's taking a picture of people. It could be like opening or shutting yourself up to people— widen the exposure for others. No question about that.**

3 **Through windows I guess I see couples. Is this supposed to be yourself as a couple? You see them reflected in good light, I hope. I drew a distant room (through a glass darkly) with a window at the end of the room. I am happy to see people together looking protected. I probably put myself on the inside, it could be.**

4 **A continuing spiral, upwards, positive, never down, always upwards; it's not an easy ladder to climb. As you can see it's like snakes and ladders, oh, dear.**

5 **"Everywhere," like a boat on an ocean, like being on a boat. It's calm and rough. Occasionally, from time to time, like the ocean it constantly amazes me. That's true to life, generally, I think. Since sexuality is related to one's life, it's the only thing you can't tame—the big ocean.**

6 **One's imagination is never consistent, always changing; it's like my heartbeat. Constantly my imagination always gets the better of me anyway. I dreamt a serious dream last night; it's part of one's heartbeat, one's life. Totally interconnected, and without it we are nothing—tam ta ta tam!**

This young man's experience of life is like MTV—he is very acutely aware of visual images and of sound effects, he very much contributes to the visual imagery and to the sound effects of his environment, but the sharpness, the vibrancy of his expansive, probably international existence leaves very little energy for contemplation, or even for a sense of continuity. Encounters are intense but brief, and left to chance. The senses—both sensory and sensual—are bombarded with as much stimulation as possible, but the resulting experience has a self-referring, solipsistic quality.

He personifies the aspects of youth most envied as well as most disapproved of by his elders.

CARY ELWES

ACTOR

Nick Rason.

ONESELF OTHERS A COUPLE

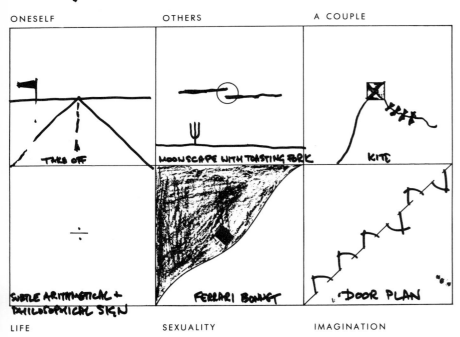

LIFE SEXUALITY IMAGINATION

1 The tendency with the point anyway is just to seek after the vanishing point. I suppose it's partly ethical training in a way that tends to dictate that sort of response to that sort of doctrine thinking. And so one always thinks of that sort of diagram. And I mean it would sometimes be a road, or because I have a particular interest in flying, be a runway. I mean one could draw a million different concepts of flying and taking off in life and the meaning of life and all the rest of it. But I suppose I'd say at this point in my life there's quite a good feeling of things sort of taking off again. Time, without quite the sort of clear direction that it's got at the moment. Because touring's so intense, the job is so absolutely clear, the work, the job, everybody knows what to do. That's great, because sometimes that sort of job isn't that clear, it can be quite shaky also. It's very positive.

2 I mean it's rather a wistful landscape just because of the way it's presented. I think, I wouldn't say, it's something I wouldn't answer clearly, because I don't see others in a general group. One sees others as an individual, each person one by one and in very different ways. People you love, people you don't particularly care for, people you work with and so on. One's concept of others, and whether it encompasses children or whatever, it's so wildly different, that there's no feeling about an overall view. Some people, for example, can't live without others.

I think I'd actually say that I'm not very solitary; I mean the mere fact that I'd operate within a group dictates and suggests an enormous amount of co-operation. It's very clear to me that I will work as a team for a while, but I am mostly with the same people—my family, my close friends, and the group.

3 Yeah, well, let's look at that, that's terribly positive. I think I'll stick with the drawing now. It speaks for itself.

4 Yes, that's terribly good, isn't it? Division. Yes, it's interesting. I mean I've just got this sort of graphical response to the line, because the two people are on either side of the door. That's a difficult one. I don't know what else to say about it.

5 Oh, well, that's perfect. The Ferrari is about sex, isn't it? That's not a very good drawing of the Ferrari bonnet—but that was the idea because it's so nice and sensuous looking. I mean, whenever, with cars and curves, I tend to always think of Ferraris—Ferrari GTEs in particular.

6 And, I don't know. That again is slightly an old graphical idea. Well, the trouble with imagination is you never know if it's there, and it's not something you can ever work out. It's like sparking the magic stick, you never know whether you're going to have a good idea ever again in your whole life. I could just watch television for the next forty years. It could happen. I don't know. Strangely, because you see many projections, t.v., etc.

Because you never know when it's going to come out, you know, you can try—I mean, I think you can certainly try and work at things that require ideas. Funnily enough, it links very much with other people, because I think one of the best ways of achieving, attaining good ideas is to have people interact, and you know, get a bad idea and you can massage it into a good idea, or from that bad idea can spark a good idea. So, there's a lot of good and bad ideas. Good ideas are a sort of team sport, they're like football. You can pass them on. I mean, I think particularly when someone's writing. The initial work is very much done on its own. It varies. I mean, there have been occasions in the past where we'd work separately but now we are trying to work as a group.

That's not a particularly good way of achieving good sound. It works with some bands, there are some writers who do work together. There's lots of people who work as a team, but for a band to work that way, I don't think so. But certainly in terms of a show or for something like that, it's very much part of the natural teamwork effort.

There is a delicate and successful balance in this mind. The products of his creativity are subjected to structure, to discipline, and the outcome is beautifully formed, beautifully integrated.

Not a philosopher, not a profound thinker. He may be a very fine writer, but his writing is more like an action than the outcome of his contemplation. A simpler way to say that he has the temperament of an artist but not of a critic.

A decent man, a reliable man, a dependable man. Even when surrounded by eccentricity and histrionics he maintains his serenity—and he is confident enough to remain on his own calmer path without worrying about being left out of the party.

Neither a rebel on principle nor a conformist. Very much his own man.

I HATE TO SHAVE

THE END OF THE TUNNEL

I LOVE HOME IN ITALY

I LOVE MUSIC

ST. MORITZ IN WINTER

DON'T CROSS

DANGER

done it and being out there.

3 Yeah, this is probably my attachment to my family. I'm not married yet, but this could be something like, it could happen soon. Not soon, but one day. Right?

4 Life—yeah, that's great! That's what I do for life. I love music and that's how I spend most of my time. And how I make a living, and how—although I cannot be right—I may not understand what I do, but I feel it. Right?

5 Sexuality! This is such a nice slope to ski, and I'm flying off it. Oh, yes, always first. This is life in the fast lane. Going down the hill first in a nice environment like San Moritz, with all the beautiful girls and the sun.

6 Imagination. This looks to me like a kind of a variation of what it's like, like crossing a street: look very carefully because you think, you think somebody can stop, but can they not stop? So before you cross it, look out, it's dangerous! And it doesn't really relate to creativity. This is creativity-wise.

Imagination, yeah. It doesn't really cross because it doesn't say anything to imagination, but

2 Others? No, this is just the end of the tunnel. It's always great to be at the end of the tunnel and seeing the end of the tunnel with all the relationships, business and social. We did it. It's out there. It's not in the dark. I don't like to be in the tunnel. It's clear. So, I love it when you see the end, when you see the light. It's bright. It's a feeling of having

with imagination you should do a lot. You don't have to be afraid of danger. But that's how I started.

▼ T H E   A N A L Y S I S

A man committed to his work, directed, purposeful, productive, and still loving what he does for a living. A fortunate man.

In his mid 40s, unmarried—describes himself as hoping to be on his way to settling down. Yet, with all the appeal marriage holds for him, he also sees it as being stuck in a dark tunnel. He seems reluctant to give up girl-watching in St. Moritz, which perhaps reminds him of the wonderful feeling of being positively responded to, as his work is. Or is he making a virtue out of necessity, rationalizing some inability to form long-term ties? On the whole, a contented man, however. Not many men make a great living from what they love most to do.

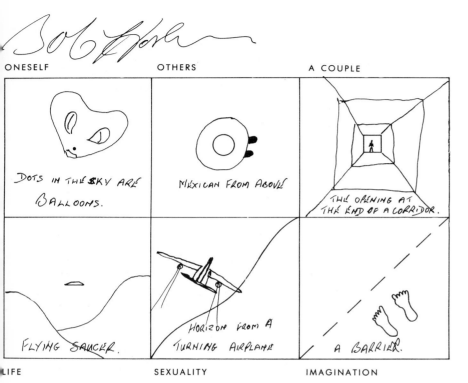

ONESELF   OTHERS   A COUPLE

DOTS IN THE SKY ARE BALLOONS.

MEXICAN FROM ABOVE

THE OPENING AT THE END OF A CORRIDOR.

FLYING SAUCER.

HORIZON FROM A TURNING AIRPLANE

A BARRIER.

LIFE   SEXUALITY   IMAGINATION

1 Floating thing going upwards.

2 Shielded thing I don't want to see.

3 The air at the end is what you are living for.

4 Pretty weird.

5 I like to fly.

6 Seems not really a real barrier. When your imagination starts going beyond that, that's when it really gets dangerous.

▼ THE ANALYSIS

An enigma! He agrees to take the test and proceeds to do his best to reveal as little as possible. An ambitious man with an adventurous temperament—a conqueror. Yet, he is feeling closed in, trapped, limited by both internal and external barriers.

A competent man, deservedly successful. Then why is he struggling with feelings of inadequacy? What is he hiding? Could it be that he is embarrassed by his success, by his visibility? And if so, why?

He may have started out in life with a sense of being disadvantaged and even with a conviction that he ought to resign himself to a modest position. Hard work and ambition eventually *forced* him to achieve success beyond his hopes—perhaps he cannot quite believe his own success. He cannot decide: is he entitled to fly, to soar, and risk a fall, or should he keep a profile as low as possible and play it safe? If nobody knows you're there, nobody will try to shoot you down.

Difficult to get to know. Socially, a shy, private man, even if his public persona is highly visible. His sense of personal privacy makes him more rather than less interesting. He gives out few clues, but they are enticing, not off-putting. Trustworthy. He will not tell you much, but what little he tells you will be truthful. Definitely not a hypocrite.

BOB HOSKINS

ACTOR

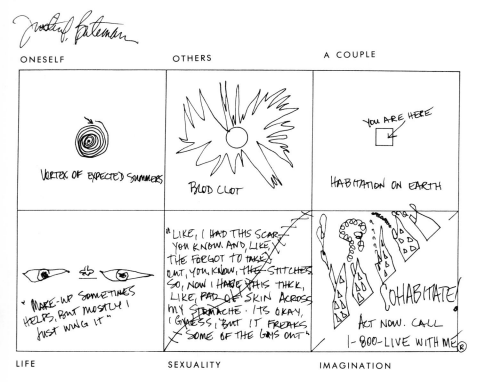

ONESELF

OTHERS

A COUPLE

VORTEX OF EXPECTED SUMMERS

BLOOD CLOT

YOU ARE HERE

HABITATION ON EARTH

LIFE

* MAKE-UP SOMETIMES HELPS, BUT MOSTLY I JUST WING IT"

SEXUALITY

"LIKE, I HAD THIS SCAR, YOU KNOW AND, LIKE, THE FORGOT TO TAKE OUT, YOU KNOW, THE STITCHES SO, NOW I HAVE THIS THICK, LIKE, PAD OF SKIN ACROSS MY STOMACHE. ITS OKAY, I GUESS, BUT IT FREAKS SOME OF THE GUYS OUT"

IMAGINATION

COHABITATE!

ACT NOW. CALL 1-800-LIVE WITH ME®

1 I guess I see myself as a disappointment, a vortex of disappointment.

2 Reaching out, but going nowhere.

3 I hate to say it, but strangulation and confinement.

4 Hilarious, a joke.

5 An imprint on your body, a scar.

6 Stagnant in this society.

▼ T H E   A N A L Y S I S

A bright sensitive young woman—but what a heartbreaking test performance. I very much hope that she was caught at a particularly bad time for her, and that she is not this depressed all the time. She saw herself as fundamentally unattractive, her life as a series of disappointments, relationships as confining and limiting, society as stagnant.

Either she was depressed enough to distort her view of herself and of her life, or she had recently undergone a threatening experience (a break-up? serious illness?) which shook her up badly.

Let me repeat: she is smart, she is sensitive, she is young, she is successful. I hope she is feeling much better by now.

JUSTINE BATEMAN

A Bodure

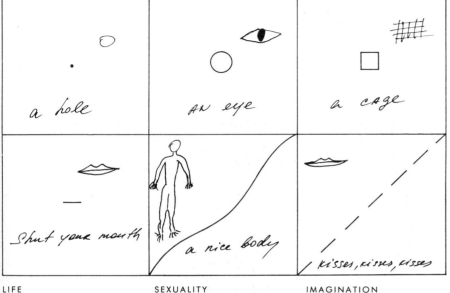

ONESELF	OTHERS	A COUPLE
a hole	an eye	a cage
shut your mouth	a nice body	kisses, kisses, kisses
LIFE	SEXUALITY	IMAGINATION

1 That each body has lot of holes, hopefully not in their head.

2 Well, I see them with my eyes, right? Right. So, that's how, I guess.

3 Marriages. Yes, I agree it's a cage in a way. I would say it is a cage. I was married, so I know. I had a good cage, but I can't say that for a hundred percent of cases. It's a sort of the design—being a square—that made me come up with the idea of a cage.

4 How would I see life? I see life these days differently than before, because in this case I opened my mouth. 'Cause I used to keep it shut, but I didn't know what I was doing before, what I was talking about. But life is wonderful when you know what you want. Well, the drawing doesn't show that.

5 How do I see sexuality? I think it's the best part we could have in our lives.

6 Well, imagination goes forever, I hope.

Not a very expressive subject. His reluctance to reveal himself is not just a matter of being a man of few words—he seems to be deliberately hiding himself. Nevertheless, he seems bitter—perhaps as an enduring personality trait, perhaps because the test caught him at a time of disappointment. He is making an unsuccessful attempt to appear optimistic, but how can anyone who appears to feel constricted, suspicious, and prone to retreat into himself be an optimist? Perhaps he was tested on a particularly bad day for him.

ALEXANDER GODUNOV

DANCER

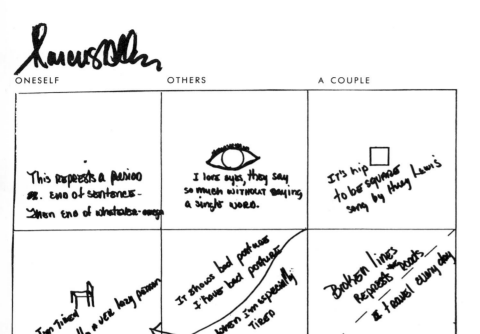

ONESELF　　　　　OTHERS　　　　　A COUPLE

This represents a period or. End of sentences - Then end of whatelse comes

I love eyes, they say so much without saying a single word.

It's hip to be square song by Huey Lewis

I'm tired - Basically a very lazy person

It shows bad postures I have bad postures when I'm especially Tired

Broken lines represents roads I travel every day

LIFE　　　　　SEXUALITY　　　　　IMAGINATION

1 I understand myself very well. But I can't draw a parallel between the drawing and myself.

2 How others look at me or how I look at others I think that that's true form. "I love eyes, they say so much without saying a single word." I had the best eyes at high school, watching people, examining them.

3 So what does that mean?

I guess I'm pretty old fashioned about couples, you know? I guess the song first came to mind. I like music.

4 This is basically me, not tired now, but I'm basically a lazy individual. At times I don't feel good about myself because I don't get up and do the things I should do. I don't utilize my abilities, I don't maximize them.

5 I don't know how the hell anyone can identify that with sexuality.

6 I have a great imagination. At times fatigue makes cowards of us all. Too scared to use my imagination when I'm tired.

Cats and babies appeal to us because of their total unabashed self-centeredness. This man has some of the same quality.

His perception of others and his feelings for friends and lovers seem to be distilled through his self-involvement.

He states, without complaint, that he is often tired, often lazy, and usually a procrastinator. Provided he is in good health, he is perhaps depressed.

MARCUS ALLEN

FOOTBALL PLAYER

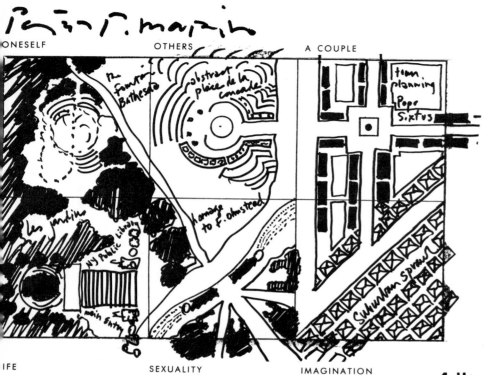

ONESELF OTHERS A COUPLE

IFE SEXUALITY IMAGINATION

the center with a lot of circles.

3 This is funny, how I view my marriage. I don't want to get a divorce when this is published. I guess I'll tell you how it applies —that is, what I wrote. So I guess what it means as I see my marriage as pretty straight and narrow. I'm a pretty straight guy and—I mean, it's a sort of one path for me. It's one road for me. I don't see marriage as ten thousand different aisles. It's really one, and it means one thing to me. So, it's pretty rigid as far as I see it. But a positive kind of rigidity. Just as Mussolini's planning made Rome the most beautiful city in the world, because he made all those broad avenues ending on beautiful vistas. I've got a goal at the end of all those roads.

4 How I see my life? This is the most accurate. I mean, I think, my life has been very good and I see it like a great big wonderful garden. It's wonderful. I was going to write "Les Jardins du Plaisir," and then I thought, no, because I should be more specific. And then I drew the stairs with the lines and thought of the public library with the gardens in the back. But it's—I mean, a combination of learn-

1 This is how I see myself, as the fountain, as the center of something. I generate business in a lot of cities and I do see myself as the fountain of design —I don't know if it's good design. I'm the fountain of work, let's put it that way.

2 I'm fairly egocentric and see myself in the center: *"Place de la concorde."* I'm not alone but I'm in

ing and pleasure gardens, which is all visual and sensual—of how you smell—that's the closest one to me.

5 So this is Olmsted, the designer of Central Park, which is a wonderful haven in the middle of cruel old New York, and this was my idea of Central Park. So I guess I see sensuality as a very closed central issue that's a big spot of beauty surrounded by a lot of very tough worldliness. And all the parts of Central Park. I mean "homage to Mr. Olmsted" is to somebody who is famous for making meandering paths that go through parks. Of course, there's Central Park, but he also did the one in New Orleans. He's really the most famous American landscaper. He studied in Europe and he laid out all the great parks in America. And he was bringing these naturalistic English landscape elements into American park planning. The English have got very beautiful trees, asymmetrical—sort of central but—I mean his designs still live today, they are classics.

6 Imagination? God. For this box I kept thinking—it's funny, I don't know how I can compare this with imagination—I kept thinking of it as some kind of repetitive unit, which is not imagination to me.

Imagination is some kind of wandering idea. "Suburban sprawl." I was just seeing it as some item that appears a thousand times the same, and it's too close together. Maybe, there's not much imagination around today, and everybody thinks alike. It's also the times we live in, the 1980s. There's a great social pressure for you to think just as your best friends thinks. Nobody can be original any more. If you have some outlandish thought they all turn away.

I don't know what it is. But I don't think we're in a very imaginative period over the last few years, except maybe for Spain. It's starting again. It's starting to leak out of the cracks. It's like there's suddenly a crack and it's coming out again because it's been held in for so long. All the great painters, musicians, photographers, and fashion designers come from there now. Starting a bit. But coming from the American point of view—boy, there's not too many people there, and we're a country of 250 million people, and we're just like the Soviets. Everybody thinks alike! At least we've got freedom. We've got the freedom, we've got the freedom to think alike.

▼ THE ANALYSIS

Wow! This man has a way with a pen and he doesn't like empty spaces. He is an excellent example of the personality of the successful entrepreneur. He exudes energy, he has global vision, he needs to make things happen, and most important, he knows *how* to make them happen.

He is open to inspiration from the past and is capable of integrating the past with his view of the future. He himself wants to be, and probably will be, an inspiration to others who will look back to him.

Not only does he have the assets of exceptionally powerful and effective men, he is fortunate in that he doesn't seem to have their usual liabilities. His personal life lacks *sturm und drang* and provides him with a safe and restful haven.

He enjoys life and wants to provide others with a more joyful one. Any defects? Maybe he could be a little more charitable with people who do not share his vision and imagination, who have to function on a more pedestrian plane.

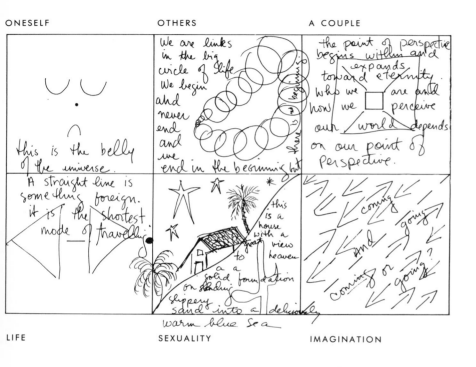

ONESELF   OTHERS   A COUPLE

LIFE   SEXUALITY   IMAGINATION

1 This is the belly of the universe. I see myself as the mother and as a helping hand, and also as a little speck in a big, big blue ocean.

2 I see others basically the same way as I see myself. We are all reaching out our hands to try not to slip and slide in all directions, as we spin faster and faster before we get completely out of control—for the big belly opens up and swallows us up.

3 Relationships are bumping and grinding, touching, hurting, feeling joy and pain. It's also finding a soft cushiony spot to stay for awhile, until someone bumps you off, and off you go to another roller coaster ride!

4 I see life as a big, huge story book. And we are the writers and the heroes.

5 I don't really think of sexuality, I think more of spirits. And also some of us wear dresses and some of us don't.

6 Imagination is the big infinite infinity. That's all.

She sees life as a big huge story book and each individual as the writer and hero of each story—and at least for the duration of this test, she has cast herself in the part of Earth Mother and is using the mystically tinged New Age language that goes with her part.

She probably is, in fact, a nurturing woman, and she certainly is a woman of intense feeling; but her statements about herself have a fuzziness that conceal more than they reveal. Her drawings say that there is an interesting woman behind the smokescreen.

Kenny Scharf

ONESELF

OTHERS

A COUPLE

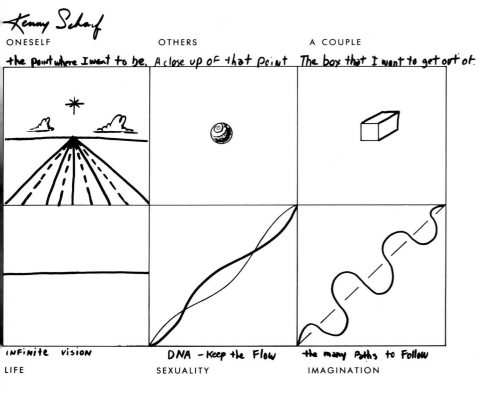

the point where I want to be. A close up of that Point The box that I want to get out of.

INFINITE VISION

DNA – Keep the Flow

the many Paths to Follow

LIFE

SEXUALITY

IMAGINATION

1 Well, if that's myself, and I wrote "The point where I want to be," I guess I'm always searching for something, not something else but the future. Something far, but you can see it.

2 See, I saw this as just a close-up of that [point]. I made it into a sphere, and spheres are for me like a whole. So, I look at a sphere as more like myself, like a whole me. So, I guess I arrived at myself.

3 Well, see it's different. Like when you say cou- ples, I didn't see that as couples, so I saw that as a square which I made into a box.

I don't like to be boxed in. So, I wrote "I want to get out of it." As how I see couples, I mean I made my life as a couple; well, now we are more than a couple. I hope that doesn't represent me wanting to get out of it. Unless, I'm fooling myself, but I don't think I am. I love this kind of psychological game. I made the square into a box. Maybe I don't like the box.

4 Oh, that's good, "infinite vision." Life, that's perfect. Life is infinite. It goes on for- ever. I mean, my life in this world has a be- ginning and has an end, but I think that your energy goes on to other things. So then it would be infinite. Maybe not in this form, but in other forms. I don't think I'm afraid of death. No, I mean I don't want it to happen soon. I want it to wait till I'm old, because I want to live my life.

5 "Keep the flow." Well, I wrote DNA, which is what you pass on through repro- duction. So, maybe I look at sexuality a lot as reproduction, and my wife's pregnant again. Well, number 2.

6 I just took it as a symbolic thing in life. You're going along, and there are so many different ways to go, and you don't know which one to go, but you have to choose. And the other different ways—so I looked at those open spaces as different doors.

That's imagination? Oh, yeah, that's everything. And "the many paths to follow" is also true.

A man of vision. He is constantly defining and redefining himself and his world, and is doing so in a creative, productive way—not in the ruminative mode unhappy people become entangled in.

With regard to the confining structures of life, (family, business, professional obligations), he has a healthy mixture of respect and rebellion.

He appears to be at peace with himself, with his family, with the world, with life, with mortality, with the continuities and discontinuities fate has in store.

An enviable man!

K E N N Y   S C H A R F

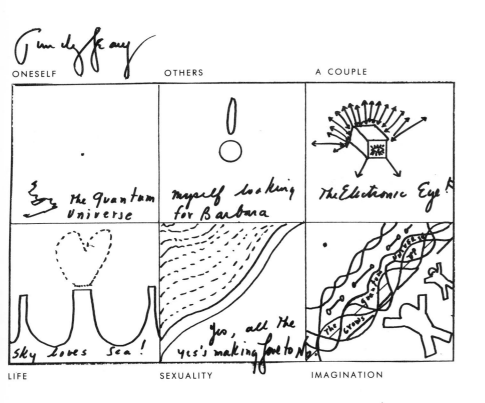

ONESELF · OTHERS · A COUPLE

the quantum universe

myself looking for Barbara

the Electronic Eye!

Sky loves Sea!

yes, all the yes's making love to No!

The grows quantum

LIFE · SEXUALITY · IMAGINATION

3 Then in this square, which isn't my favorite, square relationship, square marriage, traditional, rectilinear form of man and women. So I saw it as a screen, which is the new reality of the quantum computer age. I tried to take what was square in the traditional sense and make it into dynamic energy. I still think squares stayed in the primaries of what was given here. Giving and sending. The screen is the eye, but it is also the screen of reality.

4 The wave pattern is the ocean of life and universe, and I got a little sentimental here. I like the waving and undulating wavelike form. So I have to come back to the original idea here of the single beginning. Solitary singularity. And I just thought I'd mix it up with waves of reality and cosmic vaudeville.

6 This is the "quantum universe grows up." Nobody can read that, and you can also read "the grows quantum universe." No, no and "up the quantum universe grows." It's all information and dates running around. I take words and ideas and cut them up and move them around—the two people there are celebrating the quantum universe.

1 "The quantum universe." I'm quite sure, I was writing as it is and how I see it. I'm a philosopher of the quantum, ha! ha! It's all very still and perfect, but yet it's all getting confused, and as I looked at the panorama of the drawings, I started here with the most basic thing, which is the big galaxy and the bang—explosion of the beginning.

2 Looking for Barbara and finding her. Which is Barbara? Which is me? The exclamation point is I think when I met her everything became so exciting and wonderful.

▼ T H E   A N A L Y S I S

A strange set of responses! Coming from an adolescent, these results would suggest the kind of philosophically charged turmoil

140

found in a wide range of youngsters, from reasonably normal to severely disturbed. I don't quite know what to make of it all coming from a man in his sixties! Perhaps his thinking has retained an adolescent zaniness that gives him a creative edge, particularly if he is in the arts. I suspect, however, that his thoughts tend to be jumbled, that his emotions tend to be extreme, and that his thoughts and emotions are not always in synchrony.

He is capable of experiencing intense elation with a component of "oceanic feeling," of fusion with the cosmos. These feelings perhaps alternate with periods of depression. Even his elation, because of its extreme intensity and of the arbitrariness of its content, may strike others as abrasive, particularly if they are sober.

Some people may attribute depth and New Age awareness to people who speak like him. To me, most of what he says just sounds weird. "Waves of reality and cosmic vaudeville," "celebrating the quantum universe," indeed! Most of us have more down-to-earth concerns.

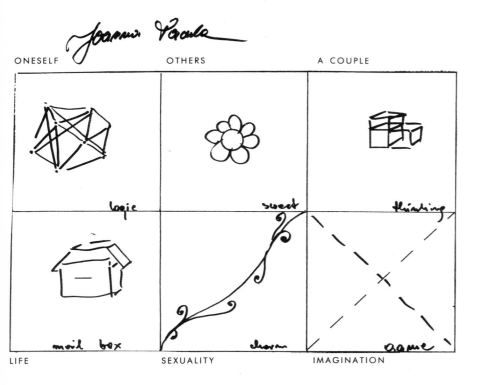

ONESELF   OTHERS   A COUPLE

logic   sweet   thinking

mail box   charm   game

LIFE   SEXUALITY   IMAGINATION

1 Well, I think in that sense, how I see my-self, is pretty logical, because I'm a very straightforward person. I suppose that's what it means: very precise. I don't like to bullshit around. I'm just very logical, I guess. I think it's amazing I'm actually not paying for this. It came out this way be-cause I had no idea, and I think I do like things in order. I do like to plan. I do like to start something to finish, etc. I think that's very good.

2 Yeah, I wanted a sun, you know because it's too easy. It's like a very primitive in-stinct. Yeah, I do like people. I think people are great and love to analyze them, and I think everybody has their own fabulous side to them, even a bad person. So, I have a very good attitude towards people. I think it's true.

3 Couples. Relationship and marriage. I think it's a big thinking game how to make it work, how to keep it working when you're with each other. To make each other happy and be thoughtful and be sort of out-there, not taking it for granted. So, it requires a lot of effort in every relationship, good relationships. I suppose. So, I think it's very right-on for my character.

4 My life is a mailbox! It's amazing, because my life has been completely mad. My family and I lived in Paris, and I went to Spain. Then, I moved to the United States. So, I'm constantly traveling and constantly in my suitcase. It should have been a suitcase, but it's sort of very close. In terms of a suitcase or a mailbox, it represents almost the same thing. I think it's incredible that you have those images based on those little numbers. It's amazing. My mailbox!

Well, you see I was in Poland and I was working in a theater and doing movies and all this stuff, and I was making a lot of money. So, I started to travel. I went to Paris to buy some stuff. It was in November and in December. Martial law was declared in Poland, which was this military situation happening. So, I got to be stuck in Paris, because the country was locked in, and so I didn't get back and I stayed in Paris for like eight months, because my visa had ended. There were no jobs for actors, there was no point to go anywhere. So, I decided to go to the States and learn English. I came to the States for three months as a tourist, and my purse was stolen in New York. You know, I put my purse on the back of a chair and it was gone. So, my passport was gone, so I couldn't get back to France, go anywhere, I had to stay in New York, and I didn't speak English, I didn't know anybody, really. So, it was kind of strange. Then, I got a movie, for six months, because my friends from Paris recommended me for *Gorky Park,* and then, everything changed again. I started over. It was really very complicated, but it had a lot to do with changing places. So, it has a lot to do with changing places and constantly communicating on the phone or by mail, because I would be constantly in different places.

So, I went to the consulate to try to get a new passport, but I couldn't get a new one. Because of the change of government, no way they were going to give me a new passport. So, I had to wait until the situation got better. It never did get better. It got worse actually. So, for a year and a half, I was waiting for this new passport. Then, I had to make a living, because, I mean, I was stuck in a pretty tough country to start over when you don't speak the language, and I didn't know anybody. It was kind of fun. In a way, it brought me luck. It was fantastic. It was meant to be, I suppose, I couldn't go against it. I just went after it.

5 I do think about sex in a very romantic way, very tender and nice. Not all the time, but today, I guess, this is a certain variation of the subject. Very serious, really, very serious and very dra-

matic almost, isn't? Very dramatic. A sort of secret, isn't? I've got a secret side.

6 Imagination—"game." It's true, isn't? Because, I mean, for me it's like such a big part of my way of living and thinking, and what I do, and what my choices are, and my friends and the people I know and everything. It's imagining me with all this energy being projected around me and, in a way, you are playing games, always, in a positive way. For me, it's not a negative play with people. It doesn't mean manipulation or anything. It means being attracted to another person and to respond to her truth. In a sense, everyone has certain priorities. I suppose that's why I choose being an actress, because a part of it is to the other person, the other person's thoughts, creating this personality, and guessing and playing with it. That's what for me is also creating a character, which is great, so it's *completely great*.

▼ T H E   A N A L Y S I S

What a delightful woman! What lovely generosity of spirit! She says so much about herself in her commentary—and what she says glows with sincerity, decency, optimism, love of adventure, love of people, love of life, and not surprisingly, love of self. And all this is not some self-serving speech, some P.R. narrative put together to make her look good.

Remarkably, her intensity, her emotional liveliness, and her playfulness are combined with a clear, logical head, love of order and system, an ability to work hard, and enormous self-discipline.

She must be a wonderful actress (her profession was impossible to conceal), at least in terms of reliability, willingness to work hard, respect for co-workers, and generosity with other cast members.

She enjoys life, and I can see why. Read her own comments—she tells you about herself more eloquently than *I* can.

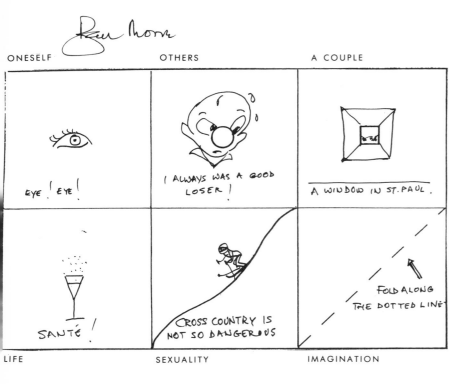

ONESELF — EYE! EYE!

OTHERS — I ALWAYS WAS A GOOD LOSER!

A COUPLE — A WINDOW IN ST. PAUL.

LIFE — SANTÉ!

SEXUALITY — CROSS COUNTRY IS NOT SO DANGEROUS

IMAGINATION — FOLD ALONG THE DOTTED LINE

1 I see the world through rose-colored glasses.

2 Why do others always win?

3 I like to be at home.

4 Cheers!

5 Adventure!

6 Very imaginative.

▼ T H E   A N A L Y S I S

A man who seems to stand outside himself, incredulously watching his life go by. Perhaps he is more intimidated by his own success than others are. He seems somewhat self-deprecating, although others hold him in high esteem. The champagne glass in his drawing represents his glamorous facade, but the reference to safer skiing, his saying "I like to be at home," his drawing "a window in St. Paul" all point to a conservative tendency, to a pull in the direction of safety, domesticity, security.

He is not very imaginative or innovative. Neither, however, is he someone who has been left behind by his competitors. He may not be a great artist, but he is a far better craftsman than he gives himself credit for.

ROGER MOORE

ACTOR

ONESELF OTHERS A COUPLE

MY DOG LULU

MAN WITH GLASSES

FRIEND

SLEEPING CAT

SELF-PORTRAIT OF MYSELF WITH HAIR

LIFE SEXUALITY IMAGINATION

1 I drew my dog. I guess she drives me crazy. I have no self left, just the dog. Usually the character of the dog becomes like his master, but in this case she's dominated me.

2 I have some good friends, and it's hard in the city because a lot of people seem very competitive or unfriendly. But this man is wearing glasses and I do, too. I was just destroying the picture.

3 It only has three legs. Well, I think it's nice to be part of a team with somebody else, but I think that there's nothing worse than being with somebody who's not right for you, and I'd rather be alone than to be in something that's not right.

4 I don't think of life as a sleeping cat. But it could be said that I get really trapped in the house. When you work at home, and you're doing an isolated type of thing, which is just with your mind, it is hard to break out of that. But still, I don't look on life as a sleeping cat, and certainly I've had so many kinds of experiences and spent so much of my time running around that it's hard for me to think that's how I view life.

5 Well, it's necessary for the evolution of the species, and I'm very sure we're all bisexual to a great extent. Because we can't help ourselves, just like dogs or cats.

I suppose it means that I look upon myself as a sexual creature. Which you can see through this drawing of the wonderful femme fatale.

6 I couldn't name that one, so that's kind of interesting that it turned out to be imagination. Because it seems like I would have been told that first and then drew the picture, but I didn't.

I depend on it for my work, and at the same time I never feel like I have enough. I mean, no matter what you make up, the world is full of stranger and more mysterious and strange things then anything your mind can come up with. All I do is pick up the *News of the World,* and they have stories that are so outrageous I could never in a million years think of them. Whether they're true or not, somebody came up with these stories, you know. Brother and sister, separated at birth, meet thirty years later without knowing who they are, fall in love, get married and have children, and the neighbors discover that they're brother and sister —I mean these stories are just wild! And to me, you know, no matter how hard I work, I can never incorporate all the senses enough . . . you've just written down something fantastic about taste, you realize that you've left out smell. And, you know, it's so complicated to get everything into writing, to get everything in, to make it feel like you're alive. So to me it's always been a challenge. I mean, to me I'll never feel like I'm good enough. And that's why I keep doing it, because I can get close to getting what I want, but I'll never reach it. It's always the book in your head that's the one that you want, that you think is your best book.

▼ THE ANALYSIS

If she marched with a banner, the motto on it would read, "Outrageous!" Her strong streak of exhibitionism seems to be chosen as a deliberate stance, rather than being the expression of a strong inner need. But her exhibitionism is not, in fact, outrageous. It has the innocent playfulness of trying hard to be shocking. Much of her creativity is directed to asserting otherness, proclaiming difference. Ironically, behind the facade of naughtiness, behind the pretense of perversion, there is a solid, disciplined, deliberate, systematic intelligence, and an ethic of hard work.

In personal relations, her flamboyance seems designed to intimidate others as a defense against vulnerability to rejection—if she pushes people away by seeming far out, she protects herself from the possible indifference of others.

Problematic as they may be, her relationships are ultimately stable: perhaps, many superficial acquaintances, but a few close friends. Similarly, under a loud show of polymorphous sexuality, a search for relationship-based, conventional sexual bonding.

All in all, she is a multilayered woman who may be difficult to connect with, but well worth the effort of wading through the initial clutter.

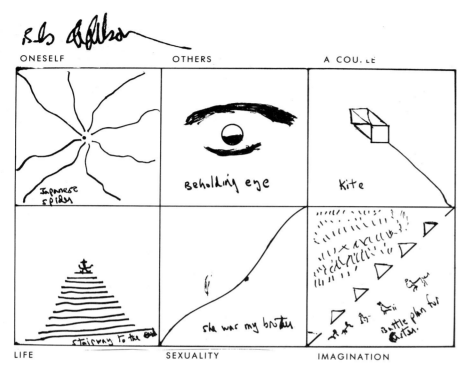

ONESELF   OTHERS   A COUPLE

Japanese
spider

Beholding eye

Kite

LIFE   SEXUALITY   IMAGINATION

Stairway to the end

she was my brother

Battle plan for
Easter.

1 **Being a disk jockey for two years in Tokyo left an indelible impact.**

2 **A bit jaundiced!**

3 **No control.**

4 **Ascension.**

5 **Or he was my sister.**

6 **I'm in the tent.**

▼ THE ANALYSIS

This man remains a puzzle to me, and I don't know whether I'm confused because I can't read enough from his test, or whether I'm confused because *he* is confused and it is his confusion I am reading accurately.

At the time of testing he appears to have been feeling particularly vulnerable, questioning some of the most basic premises of life. He relies heavily on humor as a means of keeping cool, of maintaining his equilibrium.

152

BOB RAFELSON

DIRECTOR

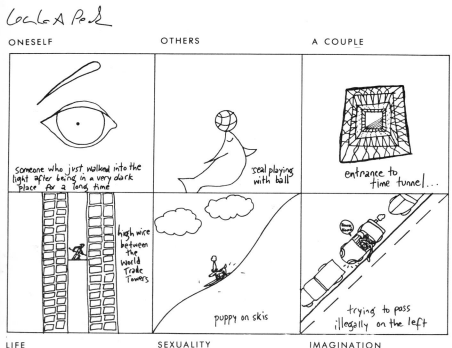

ONESELF · OTHERS · A COUPLE

someone who just walked into the light after being in a very dark place for a long time

seal playing with ball

entrance to time tunnel...

high wire between the World Trade Towers

puppy on skis

trying to pass illegally on the left

LIFE · SEXUALITY · IMAGINATION

1 Me.

Well there's an obvious connection between *I* and *eye*, but as for what I wrote, that seems extremely dramatic. I mean, I haven't undergone any huge spiritual transformation just recently or come out of a horrendous time into a glorious one—I don't think! Things are always changing and hopefully improving. The more you discover and learn, the better you are, and life's experiences are certainly eye ("I") opening. I'm on the perpetual search. And how do I see myself? Yikes, that changes every day. I have this romantic dream image of myself, dressed in flowing white robes, long hair streaming down my back, walking by the sea, elephants trumpeting in the jungle, sun setting, moon rising, I'm at places in love, and heading toward nirvana. But then I wake up and look in the mirror. I look like hell, my jeans are too tight, I'm half an hour late for an appointment, I haven't returned anyone's call, I have thirteen unpaid parking tickets, I don't know where my next job will come from, and I want to go back to bed.

But seriously, most of the time I'm pretty happy because I have a sense of humor about things, the good times balance out the rough ones, and you know, I'm doing my best. I think I treat people well, with dignity, and I don't have too many regrets.

2 Others.

This is funny. My nickname is seal (Ceil), so I

guess I could interpret this as me having playful relationships? Playing with people? Sticking my nose in . . . ? Having a ball? It looks like a child's drawing. I think it's about having fun. Every single human being is fascinating. We're all so rich in human experiences, whether our lives have been simple or complicated, fortunate or tragic. Some people can't express themselves as well as others, but they're worthy of more attention, not less.

Friends are the most important thing in life. Sitting around talking, making music. That's how we stay in touch with that we're doing on this crazy planet. I'd do anything for my friends. They know who they are! I love them very, very much.

3 Relationships.

"The time tunnel." You know, I believe that the important relationships in our lives are destined. I think it's very conceivable that our souls evolve, eternally, going from one incarnation to another, and that we keep going through time with the people who are important to us in our journey. I have such a sense of knowing certain people before, of the connection being stronger than a brief, temporary, and completely random association. So maybe that's what this drawing is about.

You know, in relationships I consider myself quite experienced, but with no authority. I don't have the answers. Each one is different. In couples, there is always one person who holds the power, but then it can flip. If it stays the same for too long, it's not interesting anymore. It can flip every day sometimes.

I have another fantasy about settling down and being in love forever and ever, but that hasn't materialized. There should be a question about fantasies in this test. Anyway, love makes the world go round, definitely.

4 Life.

I love this drawing. This is ridiculous. The poor guy looks so diligent, like he's working on an assembly line, but he's on a high wire! But life is like walking a tightrope. Anything can happen, and it does. You think you're all set, and then something you couldn't have foreseen in your wildest dreams hits you. But I love that. If it weren't so risky, so unpredictable, it wouldn't be so incredibly fascinating. You need a lot of skill to stay up there, especially as a performer. But you've got to catch yourself—nobody's going to be there. They might be busy that day.

5 Sexuality.

Um, this drawing is so silly that I think the only

comment I would like to make on the subject is that, fortunately, I made it through a rather strict up-bringing with a pretty healthy outlook about this.
6 Imagination.

Well, this driver is trying to get out of the traffic, out of the mainstream. That happens to be the way I drive, but, there's a metaphor somewhere I'm sure.

I live in my imagination. People sometimes think I'm spacey because I'm tripping out on an idea, on a different adventure entirely. This can be danger-ous when you're sitting in an important meeting. Then, I overcompensate by getting serious and using as many big words as I can think of. But with-out allowing for a full life of the imagination, I think we would all *perish*.

▼ T H E   A N A L Y S I S

When people describe themselves, or when they interpret their own dreams or drawings, their descriptions and interpretations are influenced by their needs, by their fears, by their ambitions, by their ideals—in short, by their personality. Therefore, to a psychologist, people's self-interpretations are material that cries out for interpretation.

Our subject here has such a clear and uncluttered view of herself that she makes my job superfluous. She is an intelligent, creative, articulate woman with a sense of humor that gives her strength and perspective. She can feel vulnerable and precarious at times, but she turns even her unsettled feelings into opportunities for open-ended curiosity and adventure. And, furthermore, she comments so frankly and fully on herself that I can do no better than urge you to read what *she* says.

ONESELF | OTHERS | A COUPLE

The clown I've been playing for years! (JOKER)

The Clown that I am very soon to be! (JOKER)

The people that I unfortunatley have the pleasure of working with!

The Quest for wisdom of freedom and enlightenment.

The love that I have for people who are True.

The love that I have for people who are not.

The path I travel

Hopefully with the one I love.

FOOTPRINTS IN LIFE

LIFE | SEXUALITY | IMAGINATION

1 I don't like it. Well, some of it.

1 and 2 I think everybody is a combination of the first and the second. We've had too much of the first. People see me as a combination of the two. Fortunately, I'm turning into the second clown.

3 That one is how I used to think of love. I don't agree with that now.

4 It says it all.

5 I agree with the whole picture because of the frustrations of trying to make love to someone you're not in love with. But once you've found love, the only way to go is up.

6 I've dreamed alone with images for so long but now I think I see someone who dreams what I dream and who does with imagination what I do.

▼ THE ANALYSIS

The first thing we note is the discrepancy between the rich expressiveness of the test drawings and the paucity of his comments —an artist, all right, but not a writer. Is his talent in drawing or is he a musician who can also draw?

Next we notice his ups and downs in mood and his tendency to divide people into good guys and bad guys with not much in between.

Is he a bitter man who has a core of sweetness inside him? Has life kicked him around in ways he considers unfair? He reminds me of the flower children of the Woodstock generation. But isn't an angry flower child a contradiction in terms? Well, if it is, let it be—that's how I see him: an angry flower child.

JULIAN LENNON

SINGER/COMPOSER

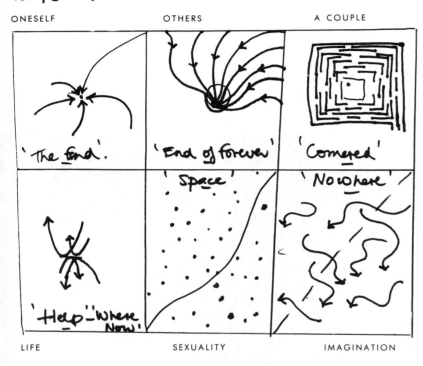

Tony Scott

ONESELF	OTHERS	A COUPLE
'The End'.	'End of forever'	'Cornered'

LIFE	SEXUALITY	IMAGINATION
'Help'—"Where Now"!	'Space'	'Nowhere'

1 I see myself as being very complex.

2 We have to live and let live.

3 Relationships seem to me very, very difficult.

4 My life is the best life. Today is today, and tomorrow another day, never knowing what I'm going to be doing next.

5 Sexuality is the only thing which stays constant in one's life. It's the best!

6 Nothing is original anymore.

▼ T H E   A N A L Y S I S

There is a puzzling contradiction in this test record. On one hand, the drawings are those of a competent, rather well-organized, effective man, while on the other hand his words point to someone who feels disillusioned, tired, pessimistic, perhaps bitter. His first four drawings are labeled "The End," "End of Forever," "Cornered," and "Help."

Under the circum-
stances, his saying
"My life is the best
life. Today is
today, tomorrow
another day, never
knowing what I'm
going to be doing
next" suggest not
freedom but pain-
ful uncertainty.

    I think he says
"sexuality is the
only thing which
stays constant in
one's life—it's the
best," not because
his sexuality is un-
usually high-
pitched, but be-
cause sexual activ-
ity provides
periods of intense
concentration and
therefore of escape
from unpleasant
states.

TONY SCOTT

ONESELF   OTHERS   A COUPLE

· universe	○ globe (earth)	radiation
— desert	mountain	geometry

LIFE   SEXUALITY   IMAGINATION

1 I suppose I just see life as not from a certain little point but just in this kind of immensity. And I don't think I'm too self-conscious or self-centered, so I see it more like a horizon.

2 Yeah. I'm supposed to see a lot of others, and I think I like to work with people. That's probably part of the fact that I always have a good relationship with an orchestra. And in a way it's because when you are writing music, when you are composing, you are basically always by yourself, and so when you finally are working with an orchestra, it's some kind of relief. It's nice to have the presence of human people. It's interesting because even if I'm working with electronics like the synthe, like over the last few years—. I like to work electronically, but still with people we can just blow an instrument open: you will see it's not only keyboards, so they are always human, and I treat technically the orchestration of the electronic, I treat that more like a chamber music instead of only machines. When I have ninety to a hundred people to conduct, to work with, it's always "one,"

even if there are sometimes a lot of problems like, you know, in different countries (like in Italy, no great discipline). But still it is one, it's the "one" feeling that's left.

3 That's couples. I always liked the other sex all my life so I suppose radiation is like attraction, kind of burning.

4 That's life. It looks like a very, very pessimistic form of life but no, I don't think so. My father was very pessimistic so I have some kind of problem of contrary—but still it's life. Especially now it's still a little bit scary in a way because you don't know: some crazy guy can push the button and everything explodes and that's the end. Also you feel that people should be more and more wise, and it looks like the contrary. It's the same thing when we invent one thing to cure people, at the same time a new disease comes. There's never really a solution to be happy; and people could be really happy in the world: we have everything but still there is more and more terrorism. Everything increases: we have a progress—improvement of the mind in a way, in technique, technology—and on the other side we have this kind of black plague coming back. Maybe a regression in a way.

I don't know. It's just very strange: it looks like, one, we are making improvement about the way of life, just the intelligence, try to cure sickness, and on the other side, there is some kind of rebounding sense at the same time, so we are not really better than the Middle Ages. So maybe that's why. I try to justify in my mind.

5 Well, I suppose to go to a peak: I like mountains. I like nature. I like to climb. At the peak I finally find the ultimate ecstasy. Just fanaticism in love is nice.

6 Well, I suppose the music and the mathematics are quite close. Just geometry seems to be a normal way to see. It could be a theorem, and it's a very interesting thing, but you see actually it's you who should make a comment on it because it seems to me very pompous to explain your own.

I thinks it's because I'm decisive in my work. I'm meticulous. I don't know about this time, but they say the piano is supposed to be organized. I can work if my place is real—and I see some people can just work and work in the middle of absolute chaos, but I cannot do that. What can I do, what can

I say more? For my music and for my imagination I need peace and order.

A man of paradoxes that hold together in a delicate balance. His disclaimers notwithstanding, he *is* self-conscious and self-centered, yet he is acutely aware of a whole world out there, which he fears, and loves, and wants to please, and resents, all at once.

With others, he is aloof and needy at the same time. He tries to reconcile the wish to command and dominate with the wish to elicit cooperation by drawing on affectionate ties. Not much to go on with regard to romantic and sexual life: perhaps he is reluctant to reveal much. Could he have a view of women that is limited to seeing them as instruments of pleasure?

As the center of an active, successful life, there is a sense of aridity, of isolation, of precariousness. Precisely because he has to combat chronic fearfulness, he is a brave man: he grits his teeth and lives as if he is *not* afraid.

His music (in this case, the subject's profession could not be concealed) provides an excellent compromise between temperament and logic, between the pull of randomness and mathematical order. His art and his craft give him a haven where he is competent, gratified, satisfied—where all the strands of a complex personality join in dynamic harmony.

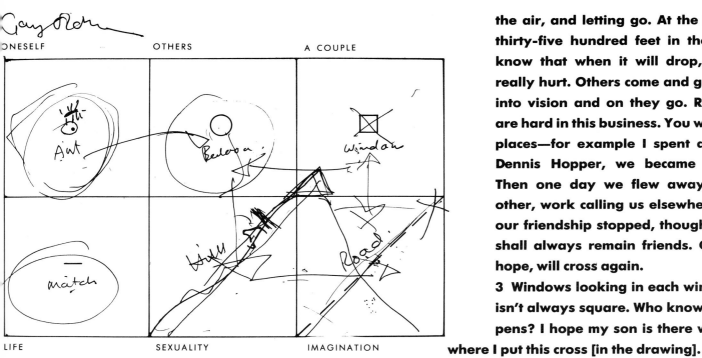

ONESELF   OTHERS   A COUPLE

Awt

Below

Window

match

hill

Road

LIFE   SEXUALITY   IMAGINATION

1 I guess we are all trodden over with love and shit. Everybody is on the line, so one always has to look over one's shoulder. We're trying to find our own way. So, anyhow, here is my contribution to the arts.

2 You have to hold on; if not, you'll drop. Life is trying to hold on to the string three hundred feet in the air, and letting go. At the moment I'm thirty-five hundred feet in the air, and I know that when it will drop, well it will really hurt. Others come and go, they float into vision and on they go. Relationships are hard in this business. You work, change places—for example I spent a while with Dennis Hopper, we became very close. Then one day we flew away from each other, work calling us elsewhere and then our friendship stopped, though I know we shall always remain friends. Our paths, I hope, will cross again.

3 Windows looking in each window. Which isn't always square. Who knows what happens? I hope my son is there with me, just where I put this cross [in the drawing].

4 Am I a match for anyone? Come on, baby, light my fire! A match for life. Pretty confused by that one.

5 It's not a hill. It's an upward climb, a hardship, an adventure, and at the top of the hill, top of the mountain which I'm climbing, it's heaven. Sex is connected; it's at the top of what I'm climbing.

6 You need imagination, a lot of it. Did I do the right thing? I'm never satisfied, never complacent.

All things I do in movies is always work in progress. The end continues forever. Perfection in work is never ending. I overuse my imagination for my job, all the time imagining I'm someone else: his habits, his path, his life.

▼ THE ANALYSIS

This man seems to be chronically dissatisfied. In the service of his craft, his dissatisfaction and insecurity operate as assets: he is always striving for better work, is never completely satisfied with the end product, and is always worried about the durability of his success. Uncomfortable as these feelings are, at least they motivate him to produce better work, to strive for excellence and perfection.

With regard to his personal life, on the other hand, these personality traits are most likely not beneficial. Yet there is nothing in his test responses to suggest that he is either unpleasant or objectionable in any way.

My advice to him:

Please try to enjoy your success, and remember that those around you probably like you a great deal more than you might think.

GARY OLDMAN

ACTOR

THE BEGINNING.

A cow searching for grass

Different opinions.

The choice is yours.

nothing, nothing at all.

EMERGENCY EXIT

LIFE   SEXUALITY   IMAGINATION

1 It is very strange how all the other drawings are very full and crowded with meaningful or less meaningful things—this one is very empty, no connection between the points. Firstly, each point represents an amount of being, information of different things, of feelings which are not directly connected to each other. There is no beginning and there is no end. No road, no path; there are many elements superficially alike but also very contradictory, one from another. With time they will became one color. All these points will maybe be so close to each other that they will be one and fill the whole square: one color only will fill the square.

2 "A cow." Around the cow are the obstacles of life—everyone is searching for the grass. There is some around but not fresh enough. She has to confront these obstacles, or leave them behind. She sometimes neutralizes them. It's easy to catch the grass because it's all over, but you have to go further, because in a while the grass will get better if you do so. Through the choice of animals, I guess the others are not too threatening. You can pat the cow, ride it, but if it's eating your grass, you're going to eat the cow!

3 Different needs, different roads—a couple tries to make their roads parallel but the road is not the same, they are going towards the same but it's never the same. One can have a road going uphill, the other will have it with curbs.

Or desires of the couple are similar, but I don't think two people are close as they can be. The daily habits give the impression of knowledge of each other's soul but I think it's impossible.

4 What can I say more? Everything I could say

about life could be true and the contrary of that could be as truthful.

5 In this particular square there is so much going on, I see half body of a man, half a body of a woman, a cock too: elements which could mean a lot, but I don't think they mean as much as they seem to. They could mean possibilities, encounters, circumstances, or fear of encounter.

6 Fortunately there is that emergency exit.

▼ T H E   A N A L Y S I S

An absolutely fascinating test performance. I am extremely curious about the subject's identity. Does she know how unusually creative she is? Does she know that she has the gift of perceiving accurately? She can ignore the obvious and impose her inner sense of ordered excitement, of aesthetically vibrant structure on the world. What an amazing wealth of visual imagery and what conceptual originality!

Her relatedness to life is that of a true artist. She finds contradictions and proceeds to reconcile them creatively. She experiences conflict and synthesizes its different elements into a state of dynamic equilibrium.

Yet she has true humility, is a reliable friend, and has a wealth of empathy and compassion. Furthermore, she is extremely generous: look at all the effort she put into a task that could have been quickly dismissed as a trivial game; see how seriously and respectfully she responded to the tester's request.

VALERIA GOLINO

ACTRESS

ONESEEF   OTHERS   A COUPLE

"SEVEN SQUARES OF THE UNIVERSE"

THAT "BLACK HOLE" THAT'S BEEN FOLLOWING ME...

SMILING FACE ON A MEAT HOOK.

GRANDMA'S BEDROOM WINDOW...

ĀLĀ

THE EXPRESSION OF CORPORATE AMERICA.

*FEMALE THIGH

AEROBIC WALTON

*NOTE: RATS INCLUDED UPON REQUEST.

SKID MARKS   POINT of IMPACT.

THE MAYLAS' DAUGHTER

HW 101

SCENE OF THE CRIME.

LIFE   SEXUALITY   IMAGINATION

1 Well, that's the terminal abyss syndrome. Terminal abyss syndrome is what I call personal black holes that follow you. You know, when things tend to disappear, like car keys sucked into black holes, personal black holes. And the abyss syndrome being that of the perpetual area or space that one doesn't necessarily avoid, but has to mutually correlate somehow with daily activity. You know what I'm saying? Be aware of it, but don't fall prey to it.

2 A smiling face on a meathook is just how I see everybody that hasn't seen the light at this point, those that will not survive through the dark ages that are soon to be upon us. When all is said and done, all those smiling faces that thought they were going to have the last laugh, and now remain beheaded on meat hooks, basically symbolize the blind path at which the majority of people operate because they can't see themselves. It's basically that.

3 Grandma's bedroom window to me has always been one of the most mysterious areas of my youth. There was a certain area of her house

where she always claimed that she could see us, looking from her window. Whenever we looked in, we could never find Grandma. So, it symbolizes in relationships, which I have had little or bad luck with my twenty-two years of life, it's kind of a view of the unknown. You're attracted to something, but you just never quite know. Until the day you die, you'll never know, as Grandma knew.

4 Corporate America is just kind of bland. There is something very generic about him. That's a nine-to-five-ish person right there. An individual who's achieved essentially what they set out to achieve which on somebody else's plate could appear to be nothing. This is a face of content. It's a neutral state of existence, to be content; it is dangerous. If you notice, there's no head or body on that face. That's some life.

5 I thought that the interesting tie-in with the female thigh against the aerobic cushion represents how people view themselves or have ideas about how they will appear more attractive to enhance their sexuality, and they'll in turn attract others to themselves if they heighten their physical being to a point of physical extreme. And aerobics have been accepted as the ultimate workout, especially for females, as a daily routine, you know, it's like Hanoi Jane has really put the grips on America. And the "rats included on request." That basically means that's your choice, you can have that if you want it—you can have that if you choose the rats, the parasites, the disease, filth, you know what I'm saying? Or you can work out.

6 Well, I've encountered an interesting amount of elements on my highway. And this being the scene of the crime, on Highway 101, I've always viewed myself kind of having an overview of things, kind of like the shop foreman, who's not to be usurped or taken advantage of. So, seeing it as a highway, if it were just a highway, there would be nothing to look at and I would have gone past. This is something I would want to spend time on or at least study. You know, the mayor's daughter of course was killed in this accident, but nobody knows why. Maybe in your second book I will provide a solution of the mayor's daughter's death. My imagination is as limited as the universe itself, at times. And so I guess I used the highway metaphor to kind of display that it's a long and hard road out

there. Well, imagination, without it, there's no thought, there's no reality; without reality, there's no life. So, it's a cycle. Yes, can I put this caption on the whole thing?

A visit into this man's mind is like spending time in a fireworks factory during an uncontrolled explosion—not easy to find the words to describe it.

He has a wonderful, playful imagination that takes off at rocket speed, zigs and zags unpredictably, dazzles and exhausts his audience, and just as you are sure he is about to slow down, off he is again spinning his luminous magic. The Grand Guignol/ David Lynch element in his humor, admittedly not to everyone's taste, adds even more spice to what may be too hot to begin with for most consumers. I happen to like this stuff a lot—but then to me *The Exorcist* is the second funniest movie ever made (the funniest is *Lolita*).

Now for the big questions: Who is in control here? Does his wild streak agree to be shelved temporarily when the prosaic demands of ordinary, everyday life require it to? Can he calm down long enough to fill out a customs declaration or a Form 1040? Also, can Thomas Pynchon write an ordinary business letter? Can Robin Williams make boring small talk at a dull cocktail party without giving it a gloss of parody?

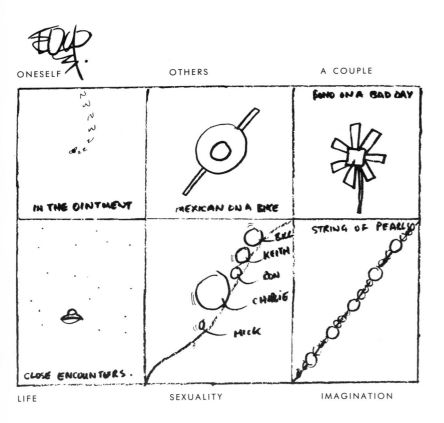

ONESELF   OTHERS   A COUPLE

LIFE   SEXUALITY   IMAGINATION

1 Outside of society.

2 It's just seeing them from above.

3 Being square is a bore.

4 Life is far out.

5 It's a roller coaster drive.

6 Imagination is vital.

▼ T H E   A N A L Y S I S

There is a philosophical system that makes a distinction between contemplative life and active life. Ideally, we should experience both, in reasonable proportion. Our subject here is light on contemplation, heavy on action. He is very creative,

with a strong component of
originality, but the fuse
between idea and action is
short and direct—perhaps
because he is afraid that a
stone that stops rolling will end
up gathering too much moss.

   He has a powerful, creative
imagination, but he is so
invested in being far-out, so
afraid of being square that he
deliberately ignores rules of
moderation and refuses to
learn from history. This
spontaneity may be serving
him well in his work, but I
would worry about his well-
being if circumstances ever
prevented him from hustling
and bustling for any extended
period of time. On the other
hand, most people do calm
down a bit with time and do
just fine.

THE EDGE

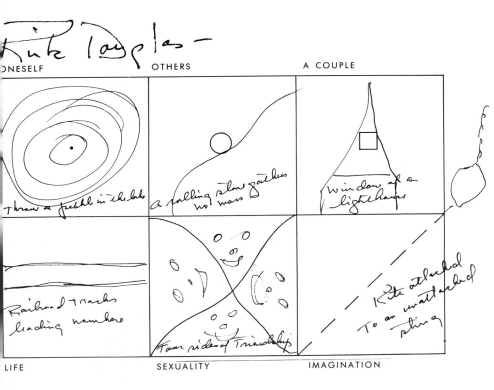

ONESELF   OTHERS   A COUPLE

Throw a pebble in the lake

A rolling stone gathers no moss

Window of a lighthouse

Railroad tracks leading nowhere

Two sides of friendship

Kite attached to an unattached string

LIFE   SEXUALITY   IMAGINATION

1 Okay. I think of my life as starting in a very small, confined area of the kitchen of my home. And then, I think of my life as a stone; then, it has the circles which widen. It started in this little kitchen and then I went to college. I went to New York, to Broadway, I worked in the film business, traveled around the world in different circles of my life.

2 How I see others? Uh. A rolling stone gathers no moss—which would indicate movement. You can't stand still in life, you must function—a key word that I tell my children, they must function, they must do something. A rolling stone is moving... there is an old saying: how dull it is to pause, to make an end, to rust unburnished, not to shine in use. You must always keep moving. It's like boxing. I would imagine the way to do something like it is not to think too much about it, but just to do it. Well, you see, everything I do is moving.

3 Now, I think of it, I can interpret it myself: everything that I do is movement, it goes somewhere. The kite goes off the paper, the lighthouse looks out somewhere: this is moving. Somebody could make it stationary.

4 The tracks are going somewhere and here, I don't know why. I just make it, it just seems to be. And the railroad also intrigues me there. Reminiscent of where I was born, you see. It's funny, because this all comes out of me having just dealt with several years of writing about my life. My house was just near the railroad tracks. I lived in a little town—very often the trains would pass and the big trains never stopped in my little town. I would see them go and I would see waiters, in jackets, tables with table-

176

clothes: sswhoosh! I wondered, "Where are they going? Will I ever go there? Where will we go?"
6 You know, at first, I was going to attach the string and then I thought, no, I like the fact that here is a kite attached to an unattached string. You know, it's faith, it represents faith, you can do a lot with faith. See if you have a kite with a string that isn't attached. That's it—*Vous comprenez?*

▼ T H E   A N A L Y S I S

This man is a powerhouse, and he is fortunate enough to know it and to enjoy it. His vision is directed outward rather than inward. He is intelligent but not an intellectual: his concern is not with how his own mind works or with how different ideas interact in a realm of abstractions. Rather, he is curious about the world, about what makes things tick, about what there is to sample, to taste, to engage, to enjoy.

His ties to people are very strong, whether with regard to family, or love life, or friendships, but there is no trace of maudlin sentimentality.

Particularly admirable is his strength and the fact that it is not used cruelly or brutally. He takes full advantage of his resources and of his surroundings, but he does not step on others in the process. He pushes himself to the limit, and once he *is* at the limit he pushes further to stretch the limits.

Is there *anyone* out there who doesn't like this guy?

ONESELF   OTHERS   A COUPLE

LIVING LARGER!   BETTER UNITS MAKE BEST COMPONENTS

LET'S GET IT ON!

GIVE AND TAKE

LOVE

LIFE   SEXUALITY   INFINITE IMAGINATION

1 "Living larger!" I feel bigger and bigger.

2 "Let's get it on!" There's room for us all.

3 "Better units make better components." Separate but with oneness.

4 "Love." Consider the alternative.

5 "Give and take." You've got to bring some to get some.

6 "Infinite." Limited only by our imagination.

▼ THE ANALYSIS

A man of few words, but not a shy or retiring man. Look at his drawings: they don't crowd the space, but they fill it. And this man, I am sure, fills the space he is in, perhaps physically, but definitely psychologically. He *will* not be ignored.

Unlike many larger-than-life figures, however, he is not self-absorbed. He includes those around him in his expansiveness, remains attentive to them, enjoys interacting with them. He is not humble, but he does not take himself seriously and goes through life with an inner smile. Nice guy!

QUINCY JONES

MUSIC PRODUCER / COMPOSER

ONESELF　　　　OTHERS　　　　A COUPLE

The perfect point

Full moon in the tropes

my country dream House

1/2

only 2 people make 1

Sun set or Sun Rise

an Abstraction

LIFE　　　　SEXUALITY　　　　IMAGINATION

1 If this particular point is myself, I see it as the idealization of a woman. There is nothing more beautiful than a woman's breast.

2 and 5 both suggest a very strong sense of romance. It ties me up to my origins. I come from the Islands—Santo Domingo.

3 I am a Cancer, I love home. It is very important to me. I'm a home builder.

4 "Half" is I think because if you are not in love and you do not love, you are not happy.

6 The abstraction is self-explanatory.

▼ THE ANALYSIS

A quiet man! His reluctance to say much is particularly surprising because his drawings point to a man of many sides, a man of many talents. There is the artist, there is the achiever, perhaps there is even the self-promoter.

At any rate, it is not because he is a timid man that he says so little. Perhaps the test bored him, perhaps he was preoccupied, or perhaps he is "the strong silent type," the John Wayne of his field. Unlike John Wayne, however, this man has a powerful aesthetic component, probably not as the originator of a new dimension in art but as the organizer, the improver, the perfectionist of some aesthetically significant activity.

His praise of women and his self-description as a home-builder are convincing as far as they go, but I suspect he is more concerned with the process of constructing the perfect woman and the process of assembling the perfect house than with the final product.

And while he glorifies romance and love in his comments, his test performance remains unrevealing of that aspect of his life and suggests a strong sense of privacy.

He is very skilled in pleasing others, but much of this skill is selectively used for self-advancement rather than in the service of selfless altruism.

A self-assured, successful man, probably self-made, justifiably proud and unapologetic about having "made it."

OSCAR DE LA RENTA

FASHION DESIGNER

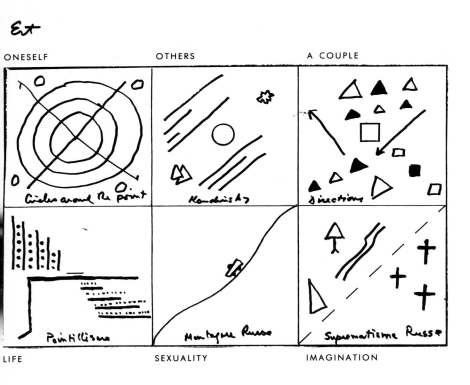

ONESELF OTHERS A COUPLE

Cider around the point

Kandinsky

directions

Pointillisme

Montagne Russe

Suprematisme Russe

LIFE SEXUALITY IMAGINATION

1 My philosophy of life is thrills. So I'm the center of my life. Everybody is the center of his life. We don't ever know that anything exists outside of ourselves, you may just be there. In general, we assume there has been history before; as things have happened, we are told that things have happened but we didn't witness them. I'm told there was a First World War; I was aware there was a Second World War, but I didn't see it, and all the events that happened, for as far as you see photographs of, could be all made up for you. So the only thing we are sure of is what Descartes said: "I think, therefore, I am." Whereas we come on earth as a physical result of the coupling of our mother and father. The spirit which is your inner self, your soul, however you want to call it, what animates you, which the Latins call the *anima,* **is something which disappears when you die. It's a pretty fair assumption that everybody else is the same way, and there has been life and history and it will continue, but it's not sure. At**

least it has never been proven to me. So, we live and assume that other people have lives and feelings the way we do. We try to be happy (a) to survive, (b) to survive in a way which is pleasant, but most of the time unpleasant, to live a hedonistic life. It's a matter of trying to do it without hurting anybody else. I help people as much as they help me.

2 I love to doodle—at business conferences, not so much on the phone, more at meetings with thirty people around where everybody is trying to talk. They give you pads and I doodle, I sign them. With a good friend, the head of Electra Records for many years, each time I would give him my doodles, and he then did an art show of all my works in L.A., and he had them all framed, and they looked good. But I do it better when I'm not thinking of anything. I like Malevich as a painter. I relate to an early Russian suprematism school, and so my doodles look like some of his things. He was a big influence on Kandinsky. He painted abstract paintings in a small Russian village without ever seeing anything —1908 to 1950. I have a great collection of his work, and most of it is on loan at the L.A. County Museum. Some of the Italian futurists were influenced by that and even the school of Orphism, which is a big influence on the first American abstract painters who were in Paris between the years of 1907–1930. They never became very important in Paris; they've sold very little, and it is now very difficult to find these paintings.

3 Marriage is a great institution. It gives you a sense of family, even it you don't have one, sense of stability, an anchor, so you are not just floating with no reason. It's actually a very strange thing because in the imagination of people it takes very different aspects.

4 This is the worst of these drawings. In a way it is a symbolic of little events which make you what you are and what you do everyday. How you live your life is a question of ethics, right? There are things, ideas, good as opposed to the beautiful or the truth, but the good is a moral question and what you are is not determined by what you believe is good to be. What you do every day is a matter of habit. If you have habits which are cor-

rect and just, it's what you do which determines if you are a good person or a bad one. And if you do a lot of bad things every day, no matter how much goodwill—if every day you do a series of things which are not just, which hurt other people, are dishonest, whatever the eventuality—your character takes that shape. That's what we try to teach our children, and tell them don't do this, do that. Giving them the habit of being good and just, all parents do that to their children and most of them turn out like not-good people, overcome by greed or ambition. Basically, if you are to relate this little bit of abstract nonsense to what you are, it's caused by these little points of your everyday actions.

It's very personal in one sense, but in another sense, if you think it's good to break an animal's leg every day, if that is your belief, it's not that personal. There is a universal code where people agree, in society, laws are there to try to reflect what is good or bad.

5 Sexuality is a very personal thing. The most animal part in us. People have different objects of de-sire "Montagne russe," [roller coaster] those are our thrills and chills!

6 I was describing what I was imitating. If I had more artistic imagination, I would have done something more original. Imagination is the most important art of the psyche because it has the ability to think about things in an important way and to think about things in an abstract way and to think about things that are not in front of you, that have not happened and may never happen—on imagination, the fantasy is based.

▼ T H E   A N A L Y S I S

You know you have reached middle age when you stop asking "What shall I become?" and start asking "Who am I?" and whether you are a philosopher or a plumber, in your own way and on your own terms you settle down to a level of acceptance which, if you are lucky, brings a welcome sense of peace and serenity. If who you are is at odds with what you wanted to become, you have a "mid-life crisis" and start to act like a crazed adolescent in a middle-aged body.

Our subject here is coming to terms with middle age and is doing it successfully. He says his life consists of a search for thrills, but he is nevertheless in a state of equilibrium where less intense but more enduring satisfactions are increasing in importance. His self-centeredness is being transformed into increasing awareness of the universe around him. He is increasingly conscious of the necessary ethical foundations of personal relations, and moral values are increasingly replacing concern with material value.

But I feel that he is also afraid—as are we all—of losing his grip on success, on power, afraid of a descent on a roller coaster which could be derailed. I think that he is underestimating how far he has come along on the road to wisdom, and that he will find he has all the internal resources to continue to live a fulfilling life.

Diane Von Furstenberg

ONESELF	OTHERS	A COUPLE
. . . . the infinite	⟳○⟳ the round about	□ the square, limiting.
△ the Triangle	the wave	? uncertainty ?

LIFE   SEXUALITY   IMAGINATION

1 "Infinite": I like this representing myself. I always leave things open for alternatives.

2 Others: around and around.

3 "Limiting": Squares limit everything.

4 Life: Looking for the peak, not necessarily thinking where it is.

5 Dunes, water, sensual; waves caress you and leave and come back.

6 Because it's like a question, searching, looking for all answers and making sure you never find it.

A woman who is sure of herself, who knows where she stands in relation to herself, in relation to others, and in relation to the world. She knows her role in life and her status in the social scheme of things, and she is satisfied with her achievements. Her self-assurance makes flamboyance, histrionics, self-advertising displays unnecessary, and her test performance is limited to the least possible output short of refusing to cooperate.

Her minimal drawings and comments reflect her comfortable self-satisfaction, but also make my job very difficult—all of which is, I suspect, fine with *her* because she is a private person who is reluctant to reveal her soul to strangers.

DIANE VON FURSTENBERG

FASHION DESIGNER

Robbie Robertson

LIFE	SEXUALITY	IMAGINATION

Listen To The Invisible Soul · SHield of Destiny · HEARTBEAT STREET

Reflection of Yesterday · Love in The Third Dimension · Levitation A Life out of Balance

ONESELF	OTHERS	A COUPLE

1 This is a reflection of my work. And the thing about music is that you try to get the most out of yourself, the most of what you can do to dig deep down to pour your soul out, to express it the most successfully possible. So, I probably am pleading with myself to do it.

2 I don't know why I did that. It's a shield you hold to protect yourself. I was just talking to a lady, just before you got here, on the phone. She's American Indian, a wonderful painter (there is one of her paintings just in front of me, a beautiful Indian holding a shield with very strong ideas). She's preparing this exhibition and she is doing a portrait of me. So, she called to ask if she could paint me with yellow eyes: it's a sign of warriors. And she also asked if she could paint me holding a shield. I don't mind all these things; they all have some kind of meaning that I don't yet understand. And getting off the phone from her, I saw the circle that I made into a shield. The colors, of course, have a signification, but I haven't studied them, but here, that's kind of a sunshine, plus the yellow eyes; these are all symbolic.

3 I just saw this as a drum and this the mallet, the heartbeat. Then, "heartbeat street" came to my mind. I drew the street. I might have been looking at this thinking of that. But that's what it is. My mother is an Indian. When I was a kid growing up, in the summer she would take me to the reserve in Canada, the Sixth Nation Indian Reservation. So, I guess I have this very strong thing about looking and just feeling. In this country, where everything seems to have a balance of life, everything has its own proportion and, as time goes by, they are more disturbed than ever, when I think about life, I think of sadness. It's on my mind. Lately, I've been trying to help the Indians through my work.

4 Symbolic things remind me of my past. That's why I put "Reflection of yesterday." Unfortunately, I don't speak Indian. There are so many dialects. My mother was a Mohawk Indian from the Sixth Nation. Anyway, this looks like a pyramid.

Maybe it's the past life.

5 "Love in the third dimension." Well, it's very experimental to me, it looks very enjoyable. I have no idea what it means. I just did the first thing which came to my mind.

6 Imagination is the key to life, but it's almost one of the most dangerous. It also gets up into all of our troubles. Levitation, I guess, is a part of my imagination. I see it in two ways: such a wonderful gift and also a sort of yin/yang.

▼ THE ANALYSIS

A turbulent soul in search of serenity, a search that frustrates him because there is a part of him fascinated by the turbulence and reluctant to part with it. Furthermore, his expressiveness is in the realm of tone, color, rhythm—not in the form of verbal, ideational analysis—and is therefore unsuitable for arriving at conclusions that provide cognitive answers.

Serenity for this man depends on his feeling at one with a group of people, or with an ideal or ideology—which in itself could be a problem because he has a mind that values cool, logical thinking and is suspicious of emotional intensity.

I do not see a move toward the resolution of his inner restlessness. Fortunately,

artistic expression often depends on the successful transmutation of the kind of tension apparent in this test record.

ROBBIE ROBERTSON

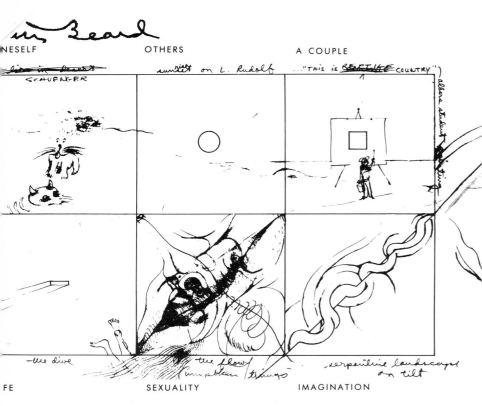

NESELF OTHERS A COUPLE

SCAVENGER   unriitt on L. Rudolf   ..."THIS is REPTILE COUNTRY"

—the dive   the flow/ unspoken things   serpentine landscapes on tilt

FE   SEXUALITY   IMAGINATION

1 It reminds me of Kenya where Bob Rafelson was shooting his film on Burton and Speke. So, firstly this is sentimental, and it also reminded me of a lion's nose.

2 I have actually photographed Lake Rudolf in my book *Eyelids of Morning: The Mingled Destinies of Crocodiles and Men.* I do tend to look at others optimistically.

3 It could be an artistic vision: too much of them is too much. Expanding on the Joseph Alber's classes—my teacher for four years.

4 Taking a dive in Lake Rudolf. The Africans had reinforced the deck with cement

and I slipped and totally ripped my face off.

5 I can't make any sense out of that.

6 If this is imagination, mine is constipated. It's a failure, repetitions; it just doesn't seem to succeed for me.

▼ T H E   A N A L Y S I S

I am surprised at his characterizing his imagination as "constipated." His drawings contradict him and reveal a very vivid imagination in the service of a very creative man, a man with real talent for

disregarding limitations imposed by habit, for transcending conventional classifications, and for synthesizing usually disparate elements into dynamic and aesthetically pleasing and exciting combinations.

He underestimates himself quite regularly, I suspect. I have no idea about his degree of success, but surely he is not unknown. Still, I think his kind of modesty or humility tends to color others' perception of him and results in his getting less credit and fewer rewards for his work than he deserves.

ABOUT THE AUTHOR

Alix Goldsmith was born in France in 1964. Half English and half French, she lives in Mexico and in Paris, and spends time in New York and Los Angeles. Ms. Goldsmith is a freelance photographer. *Celebritest* is her first book to be published in the United States. Her previous book, *80 Divas sur le divan,* was published in France.

ABOUT THE PSYCHOLOGIST

Dr. Michel Radomisli completed doctoral and postdoctoral studies in psychology in New York City. He has a private office practice of psychotherapy and also contributes to the training of psychiatrists and psychologists at Cornell University Medical College-New York Hospital. Dr. Radomisli has two terrific sons.